GW00865765

Wheelsagiey

riding the rim of an alternate reality
freewheeling through parallel worlds

cycling chronicles and short stories

Revision February 2121

Euan Ross

Rickshaws by the Buriganga River, Dhaka. Image - the Author

Wheelsagley

The stories in 'Wheelsagley' are sourced from the 'Lombok Letters' (1999-2017), a proto blog hatched during a World Bank assignment on the paradise island of Lombok in the Indonesian archipelago. The Lombok contract was long enough to squeeze in twenty missions to China, half the globe away but, fortuitously, sharing longitude and time-zone. The contrast was always stimulating.

As I rummaged through a lifetime of enriching experiences, chastening misadventure and adrenaline fuelled highs the 'Letters' took on a life of their own. After I left the island, my dispatches became 'Lifelines from Low Latitudes'. They wove a tenuous thread through a world in transition to encompass regional politics, hoary old yachting yarns and accounts of bike rides. And not infrequently, they extended into the marginalia of moral outrage and creaky metaphysics.

I have rearranged the stories in roughly chronological order. Some of the original narrative was set down in diary form, while other entries recounted on-going action in the present tense. I have regularised tense where timelines may be confusing. But, in those anecdotes where I punctuate the narrative with an abrupt change in tense as a coup de main, that dramatic device is retained.

The extracts sampled here vary greatly in length, style and tenor. Some are vignettes of less than a page; others, such as the Trans-Alps accounts, run to twenty pages or more. Most of the stories are cycling stories, but a few are not and include bike references only as an element of context and continuity.

As a keen cyclist with more road and mountain-bikes than I strictly need, I am always looking to ride, to explore. The Indonesian expression *makan angin* (meaning 'to take the air' or more literally 'to eat wind'), encompasses the joy of exploring on a bicycle. And, if I don't have access to a bike, then just to observe the humble bicycle, in all its weird and wonderful manifestations as the workhorse of the East, is a hobby in itself.

Countless aspects of modern life have been enhanced by Scottish innovations. We have 'punched above our weight' in the fields of science and technology since the Industrial Revolution. If we accept that a bicycle is a two-wheeled vehicle with a steerable front wheel and the rear wheel driven by foot action, Scotland has at least two candidates for priority.

In 1869, Thomas McCall developed a practical, rear-wheel drive bicycle. McCall's treadle (back-and-forth) foot action mirrored the transfer of a linear power-stroke to the flywheel on all pre-turbine engines, and indeed on nearly every internal combustion engine since. The design was inspired to address the obvious disadvantages of the French front-crank velocipedes of the early 1860s. Nevertheless, front cranks have survived on kids' tricycles. My earliest cycling adventures were on such a machine.

Kirkpatrick McMillan, another Scot, was credited with this same invention in 1839 via a paper published by his nephew James Johnston in the 1890s. This speculative assertion has been largely discredited; and indeed, Kirkpatrick himself made no such claim. Then in 1845, Gavin Dalzell was said to have used the same system; but again, Dalzell made no attempt to take credit or seek publicity.

Also of interest, is that the enigmatic Scot, and former World Hour Record holder, Graeme Obree used this archaic push-rod mechanism, but back-to-front, in his prone 'Beastie' bicycle. Obree's best DIY effort of 56.6mph is eclipsed by the current human-powered speed record of 89.6mph. This is partly because the prone treadle system is inherently less efficient than a recumbent chain-drive, but mainly because the Canadian's state-of-the-art Aerovelo bike was a work of genius.

John Boyd Dunlop from Dreghorn is generally credited with the pneumatic tyre, which was perhaps the most important innovation in relation to popularising the bicycle. But once again there is another Scottish pretender. Unbeknown to Dunlop, who patented his invention in the UK in 1888, Robert William Thomson, born in the fishing village of Stonehaven, had already patented the pneumatic tyre in France and the USA in 1847. After that, we left the field open for the English, even if some of them e.g, Londoner Harry Lawson who invented rear chain drive, have suspiciously Scottish-sounding names.

Why 'Wheelsagley'? Cycling is now so popular around the world that it is extremely difficult to find a concise title that has not already been hi-jacked to title books, bike companies, blogs or whatever. Every variant of bike, bicycle and cycle, and indeed every association with wheels in Latin and Greek, has been used already in some or other context.

Fortunately, there is a fine tradition in Victorian literature of referring to the bicycle as a 'wheel', as in John Foster Fraser's inspiring 'Around the World on a Wheel'. Cyclists were known as 'wheelmen' and when riding, one was said to be 'awheel'.

In the crazy days of the high wheelers this made sense, as the imperious rider sat aloft, astride the titular wheel. The extraordinary 'ordinary' design was a blind alley. Its 53" direct-drive front wheel promised enormous gearing, but this still wasn't enough to pedal downhill. Coasting a fixed wheel bike with legs akimbo must have been a real pain in the coccyx.

The advent of the 'safety bicycle' opened the potential to raise effective gearing, with a simple chain-drive linking two cogwheels of different sizes. However, the prospect of seriously high speeds downhill was only realised with the advent of the freewheel; and the introduction of the derailleur in the late 19th century allowed pedalling assistance. Effective gearing could now be double that of the precarious old high wheeler.

That is the 'wheels' part. Then we might pillage the Broad Scots dialect. The language of Robert Burns is wonderfully expressive and lends itself to the invention of compound words. The word 'agley', as in the immortal words: *"The best-laid schemes o' mice an' men gang aft agley"* has always been a favourite of mine. (Agley: gone wrong, skew-whiff, shit happens, etc. in Broad Scots usage.) And in the cycling context, not only does shit happen often (or 'gang aft agley') but after a tumble, inevitably, the front wheel of your bike will no longer be at right angles to the handlebars; it will be 'agley'. So, bearing in mind all the cycling accidents that appear in these pages, 'Wheelsagley' might, quite possibly, be apt too.

I trust that the friends mentioned in these pages are ok with that. Some accounts have been sanitised, but only a little. Life is nourished by good company and I have been lucky to enjoy more than my fair share of that.

Thomas McCall's bicycle of 1869

To a Mouse

I'm truly sorry man's dominion,
Has broken nature's social union,
An' justifies that ill opinion,
Which makes thee startle
At me, thy poor, earth-born companion,
An' fellow-mortal!

But, Mousie, thou art no thy-lane,
In proving foresight may be vain;
The best-laid schemes o' mice an' men
Gang aft agley,
An' lea'e us nought but grief an' pain,
For promis'd joy! [1]

---

[1] Lines abstracted from the poem 'To a Mouse' by Robert Burns, 1785

Contents

Image credits: The cover photo of Lej da Champfèr in Switzerland was taken by Steffen Brogger-Jensen. Most of the others, if not by the author, are courtesy of Steffen, Wolfgang Burghofer and Fritz Schwaiger. The mouse-on-a-bike sketch wears a Tam o' Shanter 'bunnet' and the front wheel is 'agley'. Tam o' Shanter is of course another splendid poem by Robert Burns – an extract appears in the tailpiece. Caricature of the author above, Jerry T.

Units of measurement: both metric and imperial units are used depending on context and location; in Britain its imperial and elsewhere, metric.

The road south to Italy. Image - Wolfgang Burghofer

Jim rides my Pinarello across a dusty Java plantation. Image - the

Dedicated to the 'Fat-tired Fabulists' of Tirol
Ten years on and still searching for Hannibal

Lifelines from
Low Latitudes

Boy's toys, Cibubur, West Java. Image - Alison Spice

Transporter

2018, Hampshire: Cycling can transport you in many ways beyond the obvious; the humble bicycle is so much more than an uncannily efficient conveyance. If we are mountain-biking, the landscape we roam far exceeds the compass of the heartiest rambler. On a road bike, for the same effort, we can travel six times as fast, exercising for twice as long as the fittest jogger. Bikes allow us to explore a local environment that is thirty or forty times greater than the earthbound pedestrian.

Our world is simply bigger on a bike; and it's better too. If we ride regularly the activity imbues fitness, almost magically. Cycling is a sport that allows you to 'empty the tank' and yet still roll home. The phlegmatic bicycle may even promote long life and happiness, although I am less sure about the first of these.

Cycling delivers on these extravagant promises. As we revel in the simple freedom of the open road, the exhilaration we experience combines the emotions of anticipation, toil and achievement. Racing the threshold of exhaustion through the countryside, it is the burdens of everyday life that we leave gasping by the roadside. We are free spirits.

But not that free; cycling in the twenty-first century has become a cult religion with an ever-changing manifesto of dos and don'ts. This can be a problem as we have nothing in common but our bikes. Even so, we are 'cyclists' above gender, above race, above occupation, above socio-economic status and above our politics. We are not mothers, fathers, sons or daughters; we are apparently 'cyclists'.

Not surprisingly, cyclists are perceived as a slightly obsessive, and therefore lucrative, demographic and relentlessly targeted by marketing men. More worryingly, we are also

targeted, in the ballistic sense, by a lunatic minority of other road users. Everyone who cycles regularly has experienced this casual attitude to everyday homicide.

Some psychopath you have never met, ensconced in a steel cage, toys with your life. The 'art of war' presents the would-be assassin with many options: he may tail-gate you, cut you up, nudge you into the ditch, brake sharply in front of you to precipitate a painful fall or simply block your path to deliver a foul-mouthed volley of invective.

Perhaps more worrying is that a significant percentage of motorists, and indeed saunterers too, simply see cyclists as a bloody nuisance. Even the best of us carries the perceived crimes and misdemeanours of the worst of us. In an era when it is increasingly unacceptable to bundle ethnic minorities and women in this way, it remains 'open season' on cyclists.

And so, we seek solidarity in association. But it is a quarrelsome 'alliance'. Road cyclists disparage trail riders, even when they have a mountain-bike in the garage, and vice versa. Sports cyclists of all stripes mock the humble flouro-branded commuter.

Fans of Campagnolo criticise Shimano and neither thinks much of newcomer SRAM. Those who don't use Strava laugh at KOM-hunters. Men get upset when women pass them, and women complain that they are not taken seriously.

And absolutely no one likes to be passed by a middle-aged couple on shiny new e-bikes, grinning smugly from ear-to-ear. But, to paraphrase the poet Robert Burns, a cyclist's a cyclist for a' that.

Cycling has certainly transported me; it's been life changing. As a remembered activity, rediscovered, it has transcended the rituals of exercise. In 1990, one of the members of the Jakarta Hash House Harriers had access to a warehouse-

full of Fuji mountain-bikes, in limbo following a cancelled export order to Japan.

The Hash is a global running club that organises a weekly cross-country paperchase, often in wild and exotic locations. I must have taken part in more than 1,000 hash runs. It was a big part of my life for 20 years until I rediscovered cycling.

We bought two shiny new bikes. Like most of my generation, I stopped cycling when I passed my driving test at the age of 17. But as children, and again like countless others, we spent many happy hours 'mountain-biking' on rugged single-speed bicycles with chunky tires, decades before 'Repack' and the reinvention of the modern sport in Marin County, California.

The realisation was almost instant. Second time around, grown-up biking is just as much fun as it ever was when we were kids; maybe even more so, now that we can go up-hill as well as down, courtesy of a lavish cluster of newfound mechanical advantage. It was a revelation, it was magic. It was a fresh and unexpected new passion.

The nineteen-nineties were a great time to be trail-riding. There was so much imagination and invention and so much to fascinate New equipment came on the market each year: ever-slicker bikes, aluminium frames, carbon fibre frames, front suspension, full suspension, SPD 'clip-less' pedals, rapid-fire gears, Camelbak rehydration systems, Garmin GPS satellite location, Goretex, skeletal helmets, and specialist clothing for every occasion.

Then one day, I saw a white and pink Pinarello road-bike in the bike shop and wanted one of those too. It was in the colours of T-Mobile during the tenure of the tragic hero Jan Ullrich and signed by Mr Pinarello man himself, albeit in a transfer. And to set it off, a small scribble said, 'Le Tour Replica'.

Getting into mountain-biking is a 'ducks to water' scenario for most folks. It's what we did as kids, but with much better equipment. Road cycling is rather different. My first road-bike, the Pinarello, came with 'sew-up' 18mm tyres. Off I went on my maiden excursion; 120psi, you must be joking?

Inevitably, I punctured a long way from home. Second time out, with a spare tubular and a wee pot of glue let to a light-bulb moment and another long walk. And so, it was back to the bike shop to trade in the wheels and tyres. I moved on to 20mm clinchers then, after a couple of years, 23mm, then 25mm. These days, I ride 28mm and have 32mm winter tyres.

Cycling replaced running as my exercise of choice, but over the years I discovered that my enthusiasm had grown to the point where sometimes I'd rather be cycling than sailing. That was a big one. I was crazy about boats, even before I went to primary school. For decades, my life revolved around yacht racing, inshore, offshore, anywhere: dinghies, big boats, cats, sailboards, anything I could race on water.

It was engrossing – building boats, sailing boats, looking at boats, talking about boats, reading about boats. Complexity and the commitment make yachting an immersive activity. It is way more complex than cycling, there is more technology, more heritage and the aesthetics are infinitely more sophisticated.

Even so, and while I still follow my first love, most days, you will find me cycling. Perhaps the real change is that all my sailing was competitive, nauseatingly competitive, often literally so. On the bike, I have no desire to race, I don't compete. My only yardstick is exhaustion, and that, for me, is just wonderful.

The rediscovery of cycling was an immediate success, but it only became an obsession when I broke my ACL and had to follow a 6-months rehab programme with cycling 'front and centre'. My bikes have since become an essential element in the physical therapy of multiple rehab programmes over the years. Effort is readily calibrated, and progress can be monitored.

What was not immediately obvious was the incestuous nature of the game. I should have known really. My first serious accident, and still easily the most impressive, was on a bicycle; to be more precise, a handed-down, powder-blue tricycle, by coincidence the exact hue of my current, Look Aero-light road-bike.

That is the first story.

Norman with a bike I would later inherit. Image - David Ross

Deep-six powder-blue!

1957, Argyll: If I am famous for anything, it is something I did when I was a little over three years old, less than half-a-mile from home. As usual, we were running wild; my mother fully occupied with eighteen-month-old 'Baby Anne' and my eight-year-old brother Norman blissfully unaware of the five-year gap between us.

In the mid-nineteen-fifties our father worked overseas, engineering miracles. He was in Iraq with Sir William Arrol & Co. Ltd. The 'Al Samawah' suspension bridge they built over the Euphrates River survived intense bombardment during the First Gulf War in 1991. Twelve years later, it was the scene of a seminal piece of 'embedded' war-reporting published in the *Washington Post* during the Second Gulf War.

I still have a picture of my dad in Iraq – dressed in olive fatigues and a Yassir Arafat head-dress, standing beside the Land Rover he later drove back to Scotland with a couple friends, through the Holy Land and across Europe. They got all the way to Dunoon before they were stopped by a local bobby and asked to explain the provenance of the Arabic numberplate as they drove off the ferry.

In that early colour photo, he is exactly as I remember him: tanned, craggy, chewing on a home-made cigarette while biting his lower lip. In the photo, he is in the company of a group of gimlet-eyed Arabs. He is carrying a large gun and his chest is crossed with bandoleers. God knows what he was up to.

There is another photo etched on my mind. He is standing atop the North Tower of the Forth Road Bridge. A black and white image on the front page of *The Scotsman* newspaper caught the same presence – the caption was 'Man at the Top'. He let my brother and I fly paper aeroplanes from the top of that 512ft tower. It was so tall; we never saw our planes land.

Throughout his working life it was clear, even to a toddler, that the odd weekend with the family was just a small piece of a larger life. As I grew up, I began to suspect that he kept us as pets. There was nothing he could not do, and we were expected follow that example.

But as events transpired, he was not invincible. He left us unexpectedly in the summer of 1962 when he was just 42-years old. We were cut adrift to make our own way in a much-altered world. We were on holiday when Father died, but he was still commuting to the bridge-site, supervising the spinning of the suspension cables. The last shuttle to pull the final loop of steel wire across the Forth Estuary was decorated with the Red Ross dress tartan. That remnant still hangs, framed, in my office.

Returning to 1957: Norman and I are off to the 'wee shop' for the 'messages' on my soon-to-be-famous blue tricycle. As usual, I am pedalling with my chubby, already scarred, little knees bobbing up and down and a thick platinum fringe covering my eyes. Norman is standing on the treads between the back wheels and calling the shots. He is probably wearing a cowboy hat and brandishing a silver Colt 45 cap-pistol. I can visualise this precisely as there is a contemporary snapshot of just such a division of labour.

At the pier-house, Norman goes into the shop. Little Euan, lost in a daydream, pedals on down the greenheart deck and disappears over the side just by the old cargo derrick. Fortunate perhaps, as riding off the pier-head would have

resulted in almost certain death. The pier is about 12 feet above the waterlevel, and I take to the air like a paratrooper, still pedalling. Blessedly, the tide is not right-out, and the divine waters of the Holy Loch cushion my fall.

This is one of my earliest memories, swallowing cold salt water and looking up at the towering masonry of the pier. A small cowboy is peering down at me and exhorting me to greater efforts in the language of his father: "*Attaboy, Euan; come on boy, you can do it boy*" – ad nauseam.

After a short interval, another face appears by the old derrick; it's Mr Ferguson, the Pier Master. He is wielding the 'Giant's Boathook', a three-metre-long ash spar, tipped with a great bronze spiked hook. It must weigh at least 50lbs. It has been lying on the pier for decades. Like King Arthur's Excalibur, it has waited patiently, prepared for a situation when sufficient adrenaline can be summoned to wield it.

During the time taken to convoke these images, I have been steadily making progress towards the shore in the same uncoordinated doggy-paddle that I still depend on to this day. By a logical corollary of the tide not being right out, is not right-in either and thus the distance to be covered is not very far. But even so, as the minutes tick by, the struggling child remains tantalisingly out of his depth.

As I run out of puff, my blond thatch dips beneath the surface – just as the seabed rises to meet my scuffed red sandals. As an evolving amphibian, I am now running out of time. Then I feel the reassuring punt of Excalibur's hook up my backside and my knees touch the crunchy gravel bottom.

I emerge bedraggled and dripping, and a little bit shell-shocked, oblivious to the thin applause from the small crowd now gathered above me. I am far too upset about the fate of my bike to take a bow just yet. There is no ladder on this side of the pier. I squelch off disconsolately along the shore, looking for a way up. The steps I remember leading up and over the seawall seem to be miles away.

At this point, my sense of purpose begins to wander and, at last, I start to cry. It's an eternity, but eventually I struggle up the old stone treads onto the road. I am greeted, matter-of-factly, by my brother. He brings the reassuring news that Mr Ferguson will recover the trike when the tide goes out.

My close friends might observe that I learned nothing from that experience. Norman didn't learn anything either, as another incident later that summer, illustrates. My gregarious brother had gone to visit Mr Weir, as he often did, for a 'blether'. Little Euan was once again unsupervised, perched on the old higgledy-piggledy wrought iron fence by the roadside, watching the passing traffic and swinging his fat little legs.

Norman reappears, skipping absent-mindedly down Mr Weir's well-tended garden path to find the trike parked where he left us. Of his wee brother, there was no sign.

Almost inevitably, I had toppled backwards over the seawall. It was a fair distance to fall; especially backwards and onto one's head. The tide was out, and in any case, the water was only ever a few inches deep at that point. My salvation on this occasion was big pile of garden refuse, dumped by the fastidious gardener across the road.

Then, in the autumn, my mother received a telephone call from the headmistress of the local primary school. It seems I had accompanied Norman for a mile-and-a-half along the main road to Rashfield School but was now too tired to cycle back.

I gleaned everything I know about sibling responsibility from my brother. Some years later, we built a magnificent, ship-rigged raft from an old stepladder, a couple of fencing stobs and chunks of polystyrene fridge insulation. Sadly, this vessel

would not support the weight of any one of the enthusiastic members of the design team.

Although the wind was brisk and slightly offshore, and although it was still April and the sea would only have been a few degrees above freezing, we set my sister Anne adrift on this device, in the manner of Laika, the first dog in space. The raft sailed well, and we had to run to keep up with it, steering with a yoke from the shore made from an old braided-cotton clothesline. This flimsy tether skipped satisfyingly across the grey, choppy water; snagging taught from time-to-time over occasional rocky outcrops. There is something about such projects, borne on youthful enthusiasm, which can never be recreated in later life, when we no longer source materials through scavenging.

Later we transferred one of the three masts to my go-kart. The mainsail was cut from a faded pink damask drape. There were occasions when, predictably, it came close to 'curtains' for the intrepid pilots too. We took turns to hurtle along the shore-road in the disturbed air of the hill-foot. Boys being boys, we were emboldened by a tourist with a camera to perform reckless two-wheeled slam-dunk manoeuvres in the gusts.

It was a fine bogie. Steered with a rigid pram handle rather than string, we could drive it with the precision of a rally car, one handed. Our makeshift land yacht was a consuming diversion, until we mounted the rig on the less-stable platform of my bicycle. That final development frightened us all half to death; so, we retired to the shed and built firearms with aluminium aerial tubing and black gunpowder.

Euan (trike pilot) and Norman, Kilmun, Scotland. Image - David Ross

13

Where even the fish use tricycles

1990, West Java: Jakarta is a big town; in fact, it's a very big town. The metropolitan area is home to more than 30 million people, all living on top of one another. This teeming mega-city is just like all the other sprawling, chaotic Asian capitals, yet it remains unique in its generosity of spirit.

I arrived there in 1990, ostensibly to advise the Ministry of Public Works, and immediately fell in love with the infinite possibilities of a multifaceted society in transition. In the heyday of military 'strong-man' Suharto, Jakarta was the Klondike of East Asia. But whether you are trying to understand it, or just passing through, the 'Big Durian' is an assault on the senses.

In the old days, becaks were ubiquitous. These are tricycle taxis with two wheels at the front. It is not a mode of transport for the faint-hearted – the passengers lead the way and double as airbags. During our time in Indonesia, many things changed, but the big change in the look, the feel and the buzz of the city was the gradual elimination of the becaks.

My first experience with rickshaws was during a stop-over in Singapore en-route to Brunei Darussalam in 1981. We arrived green and gullible, direct from a week-long residential course at the wonderful Farnham Castle, where the Crown Agents had sent us to learn how to be pukka expatriates. We left Singapore poorer and wiser.

Our first adventure was a rickshaw ride; of course, it was – that's what everyone does on their first trip to the 'exotic east'.

An hour of sightseeing was promised; what we got was a brief exposure to the pollution of nose-to-tail traffic on Orchard Street before 'breaking down' in a deserted back alley. Our host then demanded money with menaces. The Ross family being large as life and supernumerary, we had apparently wrecked his trickshaw's drivetrain.

We had no idea whether there was a 'heavy team' on hand, so we paid up and cut our losses. It was a very unpleasant lesson. That said, we have never been swindled by a rickshaw driver in the decades since. But understandably, perhaps, we never ridden a rickshaw in Singapore again either.

In Jakarta, the becaks were not there to fleece tourist. As the brow-beaten pilots pedalled their trade, they made the wheels of the city go round. The bicycle taxis were colourful products of a local cottage industry – dressed to the nines and bestrung with bells and whistles in a celebration of lively folk art.

The becaks gave new immigrants to the city a point of entry. It was the first step on the economic ladder. Some succeeded, some failed, and some literally worked themselves to death. But they all wanted and needed the job.

Then one day, out of the blue, the Mayor of Jakarta decided that this type of grinding physical labour was inconsistent with basic human dignity, and moreover, did not fit with the image of a modern city that the administration wished to project. This National government policy dated from 1988, but only token efforts were made initially.

For a time, even as becaks were rounded up and removed from the streets, more were being imported from surrounding districts, where they were still considered essential. But eventually, when the 'modernisation' programme really got going in the early 1990s, more-or-less all of these jangling wee works of art were arbitrarily seized, and the bewildered pilots

sent back to their home villages, chauffeured aboard a convoy of army trucks.

More than 100,000 hand-built, lovingly decorated tricycle taxis were disposed of. About half of them were dumped in the Jakarta Bay to form artificial reefs, another pet scheme of the mayor. Politicians in Indonesia often extol the virtues of artificial reefs, usually when they want to get rid of junk in the Java Sea.

The local people joked that it wasn't the absence of homes and hideaways that had caused the fish to pack their bags, but the vast amount of raw sewerage pumped into the bay every day. There is some truth in that, but when the windsurfing club tested the water, we found it to be less polluted than the beach hotel swimming pools and even slightly better than the tap water!

When the economic crisis of 1999 began to bite, the new mayor allowed the becaks back into the city, an ad hoc job creation programme that dredged the bottom the barrel. Open season for petty trading of all types was declared. This was an opportunity for bit-part TV stars and pop singers to open 'celebrity' pop-up restaurants and thus bankrupt hard-pressed formal-sector operations, at least until the 'glitterati' got bored.

The reintroduction of the becaks was countermanded by the president after about six months, on the ostensibly reasonable grounds that 'people were not horses'. Sporadic unrest followed, with attacks on mini-busses and garbage trucks. It was an unholy mess for a while.

Without a hint of recognition in the inconsistency, becaks still throng the streets of every other Indonesian city.

Rickshaw (left) and Becak (right)

Throwing down the towel

1994, West Java: The scene opens with four guys enjoying a major high on an isolated hilltop. The lads are bollock-naked, dripping wet, and giggling at the top of their limited register. A moment earlier, they had danced bare-assed in the rain to shuck the war-paint of a java-spa au natural. As darkness fell, they bayed at the moon, punched the sky and revelled in locker-room juvenilia.

But now, having gained refuge from the tempest and secured a ride home, they perch demurely on grey velour, knees together, evaporating meekly like streaking beadles at a vicar's tea party. God forbid we befoul the Louis Berger International Inc. office Volvo.

Our focus pulls back in the cinematic style of Hitchcock, to emerge through the sunroof from an opaque cocoon of streaming condensation. Outside the steamed-up windows, a torrential downpour hammers on the sheet metal shell of our heroes' incongruous urban vehicle.

Up on the roof-bars, nebulous spidery blobs resolve into a finely wrought frieze of rare and exotic machinery. As the tenacious red mud slowly releases its slobbering grip, residual gloop films the windscreen and washes the gutters with incarnadine glaur.

We draw back further and widen our field of view to frame the browbeaten landscape of kota baru Bukit Sentul, an unfathomable real-estate development, under construction 30 kilometres south of Jakarta.

Lightning scythes across the night sky with shocking violence, to bathe the scene in the charcoal and silver variegated chromatography of an equatorial thunderstorm. Endless muddy terraces of rain-lashed cassava are starkly illuminated in the cold white light. Ritually shocked, the startled heavens avert 'ionize' and weep pungent ozone.

It is a desolate panorama of restless slurry and crumbling earthworks. Leafy orchards and lush rice-fields have been erased to make way for ossified ranks of bedraggled cement palms and financially hedged house plots with a view only to a quick killing. But this evening, the bare earth erodes before our eyes to leave cock-eyed monsoon drains standing proud and useless above the wayward contours. Gravity sucks without elegance in the erratic idiom of time-lapse photography.

Pluvial perdition revisited? Perhaps, but I'm afraid all in all, it's not very convincing. Even so, the rain is falling with more force than the laws of nature might account for. It has the viscidity of solid water. Something like a firehose is visible stage left. Shit, it's an erupting field-drain, laid bare by the onslaught.

Who are these guys, what are they doing and how did they get there? It was in fact the nadir of another aborted attempt to break through Java cycling's 'North-west Passage', with the bold expatriates once again failing to recognize the end of the road and underestimating the height of nonsense.

We launched this particular ill-fated expedition from a blind summit with little in the way of optimism, or indeed alternative repatriation options should the surging floods behind us continue to rise. We are resigned to the prospect of endless sequels, as over a period of months we explore a web of blind alleys, to be repulsed again and again. It's an addiction that ingrains grit and dirt in roughly equal measure.

Cycling home on the Devastation Highway. Image – Jim Hamann Collection

Euan and Samuel, Cibubur. Image – Alison Spice

19

Java Roubaix

1995, West Java: With Jim running the programme Saturday night dinner dates inevitably fell by the wayside. And, after we crenulated the floor-pan of his executive saloon and exchanged it for a Chevy Blazer SUV, the quest for the perfect spot to start the day's escapade dragged on at ever-greater length.

Typically, at four o' clock we would still be looking; deep in the mountains south of Bogor, negotiating a precarious single-track backroad, perversely unable to double-back let alone park, debus and start pedalling.

So, we always got back to the city in the dark and, since it pours at dusk every evening in the spinal highlands of Java, even moderate excursions took on the logistical dimensions of a heroic adventure.

In this context, the term 'mountain-bike' is a misnomer. Unless you want to spend your day carrying the wretched thing, seek out valleys and confine your alpine ambitions to small hills. Wannabe mountaineers should admire the view, then get back in the car and seek out lesser gradients.

Citereup is just two kilometres from the toll highway, but this short road-link is perpetually clogged. A thousand hopeful hackney cabs have fossilized to form eternal traffic jams of blunderous competition. I suspect half of them are up on bricks. The locals climb aboard to rest their legs and chat, then they get out and walk.

This small town is obscure, but it should be famous. It is the spiritual home of the bemo or 'shitty wee blue van' – scourge of South-east Asia. Each little micro-bus is lovingly re-forged as soon as it leaves the showroom, to reappear with spoilers, skirts and flared arches, wide alloy wheels, windows black or silvered and with an earthquake stereo rocking the boot-space.

With the Citereup one-way system, it normally takes the best part of an hour to traverse an urban footprint the size of a big traffic island. We have no time for such nonsense, so I leap out to remove a line of cones and we cut through this shit, contra-flow…. right by the neighbourhood cop-shop.

Seamlessly, we are helpfully directed into the police-station compound to negotiate the fine. This done, we complete the illegal manoeuvre with the smiling assistance of the local traffic-cops. When the force is with you….

It's hot to start with and the first couple of hours on the bikes are tough. We thread a tortuous route through patchy, variegated shade, seeking relief from the intense midday sun. The trail begins to rise, slowly initially, then more and more ambitiously, to gain the high ground on the south flank of the broad Cikeas flood plain.

Below us, lies some of the finest scenery in Java: The valley floor is decked with an impossibly green patchwork of rice terraces, loosely stitched together by the glittering threads of cascading irrigation systems. Grinding slowly upstream towards the watershed, past sparkling rapids and densely wooded sugar-loaf mountains, it's about as good as it gets on a bicycle.

This section tops out at a long-abandoned plantation road, dating from the Dutch era. The next stage is a descent, but not an easy one, since the once-workmanlike surface of huge, angular cobbles is riven with potholes and badly broken up.

Thus, when we break from the pavé onto rolled asphalt it's a welcome relief, even if it's a detour that involves doubling

back. But then, after a few klicks, we pick out a promising trail, which we know for sure loops back to the main road, but which also features an enticing tangent at its apex – a likely-looking path leading due south towards Sentul. Its irresistible.

This is awesome single-track, on the edge of the possible. Our little peloton straggles through picturesque mountain villages, following a well-graded incision along the side of a steep gully, onwards and upwards. Above the cultivated hillsides, the jungle condenses around us in a luxuriant miasma. The forest canopy overhead closes in. It is dense and dark, with the full-throated chorus of a gazillion insects creating a buzz in us too.

After an hour or so, we gain the watershed to confront a mesmeric washboard landscape of endless forested ridges. I can see a long way; but, clearly, we'll have to go a lot further than that to get to where we want to go.

It's a good news, bad news deal.

The trail leads in the right direction, even though in Java, as indeed in most places, the old routes almost never run across the grain of the landform. This is also the bad news, and why there are as many philologically distinct languages in New Guinea as there are valley systems.

A long, strenuous afternoon stretches out before us to be reeled in painfully, ridge-by-ridge. Drastic mind-over-matter measures are called for. Sometimes, if you keep pushing and break through the pain-barrier, you feel great and it seems like you can go on forever. If not for that discarnate stoicism, our small expedition would still be out there.

I doubt few if any bikes had been through there recently, since, or indeed ever. In that respect, among many others, it was one of these days that I'll never forget.

Much later, we crest another scrubby hilltop, but this time euphorically – the stream at the foot of the valley on the other

side is straddled by a footbridge and it's not made of bamboo. Even better, we glimpse a motorbike on the far bank.

That's a good enough excuse to draw out the water-stop and perform the sacrament of the reviving dunk. Of course, diapered cycling shorts are something of a liability when soaking wet. Still, who cares; well, at least for the next twenty minutes, until increasing chaff sparks latent nappy-rash.

When we do at last gain familiar ground (and we have been at this quite a while already, as you will have gathered) it is indeed familiar, but alas as the furthest reaches of another very long ride from the opposite direction. Our spirits don't just sink, they plummet under the weight of revelation.

I glance over my shoulder and glimpse the pain barrier, last seen ground into the dust miles back. It is in full view, apparently darned and now dogging our heels, ready to slip ahead and pop up at the first sign of weakness. That sign is manifest in an encounter with a wee blue van, boom boxes blaring, another hour down the track near Bukit Sentul.

Jim and Ian flag-down the mini-bus and negotiate a charter. As the driver counts the money, the conductor summarily ejects the passengers in residence and loads-up the freeloaders' kit. This shameless crew leap aboard gleefully.

But there is a god. Pan, the great god of mountain-biking, a goat with attitude, ensnares the slackers' ride in the heaving gridlock of Citereup. Thus, Dave and I arrive back at our point of departure, fuelled by the euphoria of achievement, a few minutes before the back-pedalling bilkers.

That's mountain biking in Java.

'Bemo' minibus

Jim crossing the Cisarua River. Image – Jim Hamann Collection

Slash-and-burn

1996, West Java: It was early morning, but the highway bitumen was already incalescent, bending the air and distorting the landscape. The traffic around me floated on a magic carpet of mirage-bubbles. I had a clear run through to Gunung Puteri and I hit the dirt at 8.30 a.m. However, at the height of the dry season, just south of the Equator, this was already too late.

I had planned a big left-hand loop through the hills, to check out the progress of a new high-level 4WD trail that had been under construction for an eternity. It seemed likely that the Jakarta biking fraternity would now have access to a large area of previously inaccessible and probably unridden countryside.

The first 5 kms from the trailhead were clean, billiard-table smooth red dirt. Then I found that I could ride directly across the dried-up padi fields to gain the foothills – a new experience. I re-joined the beaten track for a solid granny-gear climb on single-track, embellished with several good technical sections, opened-up by the continuing drought.

When I reached the new 4X4 track, I found that it had only penetrated the uplands for a few kilometres. The fresh earthworks came to an abrupt end against a steep, scree-covered hill-face. I scrambled up the rise and looked over the crest to find a rocky but rideable trail snaking downhill into the bush and leading in the direction of some dramatic limestone scenery. This was encouraging, so I slithered back down the hill to collect the bike.

But this is notoriously hard country to read. After a few hundred metres, the single-track petered out in a small 'slash and burn' clearing. I checked out the various options from the adjoining hill-tops before finding a feasible gully to follow. Weird, razor sharp striations had been exposed by the recent bush-fires – chalk white against carbon-black. This must have been beautiful place just a couple of months ago.

I gained the welcome shade of a forest canopy and traced a braided labyrinth of goat tracks through the woods for another few kilometres. Progress became increasingly difficult, the gully meandered, and I became disorientated. I began to suspect that I was lost. Well, only 'lost' if I was still intent on going forward. In these circumstances, for some reason, going back is never an option.

And so, enticed by a suddenly more benign jungle path, I coasted deeper and deeper into this enchanted forest. Sheer, almost translucent, limestone cliffs now reared on each side. It was hotter than Hell; the sun beat down from directly overhead. Another hour passed, and I could now concede that I was truly lost, and in both 'in' and 'out' directions.

But, of course, you cannot travel far in Java, the most densely populated island in the world, without meeting someone. I broke out into another slash-and-burn clearing; this one was larger and still burning. The new path traced a line of withies across the dead ash of the forest floor, as if the sticks promised safe passage through a minefield.

A wizen old woman and a young girl with a baby-in-arms tended the scrub-fires. They were camped there in a small woven hut with sleeping mats and cooking pots – not usually a good sign in terms of likely access. But then I caught sight of an exit trail, wider and clearly more heavily trafficked than the one that led me here. Grounds for optimism?

I plunged into a broad, sinuous gorge, for all-the-world like a dry riverbed. Beneath a high shade canopy, the jungle floor was animated with capricious thornbushes and dense leaf litter. Fragments of gnarled and stunted primary bush clung to the harsh footing of the near-vertical valley sides.

Another half-an-hour of easy riding brought me to a 'T' junction with another major jungle thoroughfare. Right or left? Left would surely take me out too quickly, so I went right. I had plenty of water left – enough for another couple of hours of riding. For a moment – a very brief moment, I thought that this was turning into a really good day.

A slow steady climb revealed a flattened Djarum cigarette pack on the path and the glint of sunlight on a hot tin roof. Civilisation? Unfortunately, not; it was just a few miserable shacks. But no problem, it was still an inhabited village and the locals seemed friendly. All I had to do now was find a motorcycle and follow its tracks out.

But there were no motorbikes, no bicycles and, I slowly realised, no tyre tracks either. I rode across a small vegetable patch and found myself back in the jungle. After a short while, the trail became too steep to ride as it led me into a maze of limestone crags and ravines at the valley head. It was clear now why there were no wheeled vehicles in the kampung.

The dual-suspension Cannondale I had back then was great for rocky descents but, it was an awkward brute to carry up them. To make progress now, I had to wedge the bike in the jagged rock formations overhead and clamber up behind it, then repeat the process, again and again. All the while, I cursed the limestone, razor-sharp underfoot and blinding-white under the glare of the tropical sun.

Another cigarette packet and some candy wrappers introduced a vague notion that there must be a community nearby. Not too much further, perhaps? But by now, I was stopping more and more frequently. The temperature in this nightmare landscape of dazzling rock and stunted scrub must have been into the mid-40s. My Camelback was almost dry, and I began to worry about dehydration.

Another crest and a technical descent: Who cares where the trail goes now. I drop the saddle and go for it. Half-a-kilometre later, I am upside down with my head in a thornbush and the bike on top; not an easy position to get out of. Scratches everywhere but no injuries and, of course, the bike is undamaged as it is still up in the air, clipped to my feet.

This only happens once more before I meet another group of shifting-cultivators and again enjoy the respite of soft black ash beneath the tyres. The trail gets easier; more well-tended subsistence crops, a fishpond, a small padi-field and a peasant family sporting huge, conical hat. The locals laugh at the weird-looking bike and my torn and dusty Lycra.

Somehow, the landscape is now more familiar. I grind up another hill to a small village and look around. I know this place. On a previous lone epic, I ended up here; only on that occasion the starting point had been somewhere else entirely. The other problem: I now know with certainty that it's a long way out and the trail is evil. I get off my bike and expire beside it.

What to do? I could stay here, convert to Islam, work in the padi fields and marry a local girl. Alternatively, I could loop back left and re-cross the plateau about 10kms to the south, following the almost unrideable cobbles of an old Dutch plantation road. From there, I knew a drop-off to the Jonggol Plain which would take me back to the van. It would be maybe 35 or 40kms in all.

It's hard to get up on the bike again and I briefly flirt with the first option. Attractive as it is, there is no evidence of cold beer in the village and so I commit to the second. The Camelback is dry, and I have less than half-a-bottle of water. Its 12.30 p.m. and it's as hot as I can ever remember. This is when I discover that I have left my emergency cash behind. The wretched display of bottled water in the village warung mocks me as I ride past. From here on in, each hill seems to get harder. I pace myself and stop often.

The limestone massif I have recently traversed now rears up to my left; a protected forest in this district, but still punctuated with the tell-tale columns of smoke from local burn-off. At one point, a dormant roadside fire explodes into life and the flames billow right across the trail as I pass. The searing heat singes the hair on my arms and leaves the skin taught across my face.

As the nation's farmers rush to participate in another dry-season orgy of slash-and burn, the traditional cycle of renewal has been eclipsed. With deforestation on this scale, they lose essential water resources, biodiversity and building materials, and the vital micro-climate sanctuaries provided by shade canopies and windbreak thickets.

The trail is better than I remembered. But still the endless rocks and cobbles are beginning to tell on both me and the bike. I ride carelessly, flying down the broken surface out of control with the bike leaping around underneath me. There is no bailing out; my SPDs are now cased in limestone and the pedals are effectively welded to my feet.

I reach the padi-fields with the inside of the last bottle still wet. Now there were only 10 or 12kms to the icebox and a wonderful world of 100+, 7Up, beers, bananas and Mars bars. New earthworks and a new housing development in the foothills depress me. The area is largely unspoiled because it's been inaccessible in the wet season.

Only 6 or 7kms to the trailhead; my mouth is dry, and my tongue feels like a Weetabix. I can see the Toyota and for some reason, this welcoming sight drains my residual energy. I lever the Cannondale off my feet with some difficulty, pour a 100+ down my parched throat and revel in a certain warped sense of achievement.

Samuel on a hot tin roof. Image – the author

High-performance mud

1997, West Java: Jakarta is portrayed by Manila in the 1982 film, 'The Year of Living Dangerously', but few notice the difference. The action takes place during the fall of Sukarno. The dark and oppressive intimidation of Indonesian society during the run-up to revolution was realised with great skill by the Australian filmmakers.

We lived through similar palpable tensions which resurfaced when Pak Suharto was deposed in the so-called 'Reformasi' of 1998. However, the Indonesian version of 'Stasi' is not the only source of disquiet, and occasionally abject terror, for the population of this otherwise idyllic nation of 18,307 tropical islands.

Indonesia perches on the rim of the so-called 'Ring of Fire'. Fortunately, however, not all the archipelago 'lives dangerously'. The great alluvial plain, which stretches from Jakarta to the central mountainous spine of Java, forms a thick safety-blanket to insure the foundations of the capital city against the devastation of earthquakes.

The surface geology is characterised by light friable soils. They are low-density, high-void clays tinted red by iron oxide. In the dry season, this red-dirt endows the local trails with a hard, durable wearing-course. The dirt becomes highly polished and billiard-table smooth.

As a surface for aggressive mountain-biking, it is close to ideal. High speeds can be attained on such manicured single-track, particularly downhill. Off the beaten-track, conditions are very different but just as much fun. The uncompacted soil becomes air-borne with ease, throwing-up spectacular plumes of red dust from the rear wheels. In these conditions, you do not want to be at the back of the pack.

In the wet season, well, in the wet season things are somewhat different. Everyone who rides mountain-bikes in West Java has their own red mud story. All are sorry tales of self-inflicted trials and interminable tribulation. Mine was borne on habitual, if habitually unrealised, optimism.

Weeks of rain in Jakarta; ponderous, engorged columns of charcoal grey cloud bring premature twilight to the city by mid-afternoon. Come Saturday morning, it's not exactly a weather window, but an enticing chink of sunlight is half-heartedly evaporating a puddle by the front door.

At Bojong, an hour's drive south, conditions are unexpectedly perfect. The only constraint on the day's exercise is not apparent until I am set-up and ready to go. I am wearing flip-flops and have no shoes with me – none, of any sort.

With flat pedals this is not so much of an issue but, to make life simple, all my bikes have the same Shimano SPDs. Without the proper shoes, you are effectively stuffed. We might rephrase that: if you have any sense, you are stuffed.

Well... perhaps... maybe. As I cycled round the in-field pondering my situation, the sharp XTR cleats settle snugly into the thick rubber soles of my old flip-flops. It seems worth a try; an hour or so on the flat, nothing difficult, an hour's exercise salvaged from an otherwise pointless outing. And so off we go.

After that provisional hour, optimism displaces any lingering common sense and I take to the hills. Just as, when you wreck your derailleur and are forced to build a single-speed drivetrain with the debris, it doesn't ruin the day – it merely

changes the scope and therefore the goals of the exercise. Cycling without cleats might open-up new challenges, which might then become worthwhile in their own terms.

Or more simply, I was having a fine old time until the first fat drops of rain began to kick out little craters in the deep red dust. Then the heavens didn't just open, they dumped everything they had up there.

Now, it is one of the paradoxes of the red-mud-scenario that, as long as it keeps on raining, you can still make progress. So, I still thought that everything might still be ok, even with shit happening all around me.

But then, my right flip-flop blew apart under the strain. I fixed it with a bamboo dowel and a bit of string found by the roadside. But now I had a layer of slimy mud between my foot and the flip-flop and between the sandal and the cleat. After the other flip-flop broke, things became much more difficult but still not yet impossible. That happened a moment later.

The downpour eased, the sun came out and the red slime changed instantly to a matrix of tenacious red gunk. As everyone who has experienced this knows, the only realistic option is to dismount immediately and carry the bike, before a process of rapid accretion makes the bugger too heavy to lug. And to then carry it all the way out. No one ever does.

On a previous occasion, before the advent of disk brakes, I had pedalled on in ever-lower gears until I ripped the brakes off the front forks. This time I just ground to a gentle halt – miles from anywhere. I was on a path built along a sequence of major dykes in the rice-padi, at the foot of the hills I had recently quit.

In this situation, there is not a lot you can do except haul your 100kg ex-velocipede to the nearest river and heave it in. The exercise is not any easier with bare feet. Bojong's red mud is so sticky, it doesn't simply wash off. You are forced to laboriously dig the bike out of the mud-ball with a pointed stick. I did that, repaired my flip-flops, and set off again.

Even minus the gratuitous flip-flop component, the process is interminable. Walk half-a-klick until exhausted, ride 100 metres until mud-balled, drag the bike to the nearest stream and, amid all this, effect running repairs to the flip-flops. Repeat until exhausted.

I have seen this struggle consummated in utter and complete desolation. I have seen strong men cry. I have seen an old mate summon the enormous effort required to throw his brand new, titanium bike into the middle of a flooded padi field – on its first outing. It is seriously high-performance mud: from 10kg to 100kg in under 10 seconds.

Fortunately, the red mud has one more defining characteristic. When its moisture content drops to a certain level, it becomes hard then in an instant friable. The mud-ball turns to stone, then to dust before your unbelieving eyes and suddenly you are freed from a momentarily petrified universe. No matter how tired you are at this point, it is an enervating, liberating feeling. It means that you can get home.

Red dirt – soon to become red mud. Image - the Author

The Elysium lanes of Hampshire

1998, England. Cycling in the equatorial jungle may bring many new elements of gratuitous hazard to the noble pursuit of mountain biking, but I doubt if road-biking on the Elysium lanes of Hampshire is any safer.

On the last ride of my home-leave, sweeping confidently round a tight bend, I confront a horrifying spectre. It is an enormous tractor, gone walk-about from the Steppes of Ukraine. It is armed with a wall-to-wall hayfork. Wicked steel jaws simultaneously brush the dense hedgerow above the verge on either side of the single-track road.

Stopping is not on the agenda of feasible options. In these situations, the moment slows down usefully, and you have plenty of time to work out options and exit strategies. Unfortunately, this tantalising breathing space is balanced by simultaneous teleportation to PlAnEt DeEpShiT, which has an atmosphere of Lyon's Golden Syrup.   Action! – rrreeeaaacccttttiiiiooonnn.

Fortunately, both me and my nemesis were trying to avoid a bloody mess on the road. As I drove hard into the uninviting thicket of hawthorn to the left, the tractor driver swerved to uproot a section of the opposing hedgerow on the right, and the nearest prong missed me by a clear six inches.

When I regained the road, I felt slightly sick and detected the familiar acrid whiff of burning sulphur. That's life on the highways and byways of England, another chilling out-of-body experience and another pact with the Devil.

Many years later, I stumbled upon a similar hazard, albeit with a baby blade-runner sporting much smaller cutting-edges. It was early summer. I was whizzing through the almost-deserted village of West Meon on the Look road-bike.

Without warning, the village idiot, doddering under a backpack-mounted bush-cropping unit, stepped out of a hidden opening in the churchyard retaining wall. I was confronted with a blur of whirling steel propeller blades thrust directly in my path.

My lifeblood drained in a millisecond and quenched my vital spark. I don't know how I missed that one either, but I do remember exhausting my entire vocabulary of four-letter words in a single exhalation.

Apart from the psychotropic effects of accidentally cleaning my sunglasses with WD40, or indeed defrosting the windscreen with malt whisky (another story), adrenaline has usually been enough for me, in terms of out-of-body experiences. Can you buy it? Certainly, it would remove the incipient hazards of taking exercise to the point of light-headed jeopardy.

Adrenaline and fear are undoubtedly soulmates, but whether they are Siamese twins, I have never been sure. What does a thrill feel like if terror is absent in your body chemistry? I have no idea, but some people appear to live-out this scenario.

So, there is the question: If adrenaline is indeed a primordial escape mechanism, activated by incipient danger, how do you get it to kick in if you have no fear? If adrenaline doesn't course through the bloodstream on cue, where's the booster-shot we all need to survive these staring-death-in-the-face experiences; and indeed, the fun?

The Western Approaches

1998, England: We returned to Hampshire for Samuel's birth. Our ungenerous government leaves the children of overseas-born citizens 'stateless'. Thus, the arrival of any new family members out-of-country is to be avoided at all costs. The principal cost in this case being a hefty three month's salary.

Mountain-biking in the winter in England is a seriously muddy pursuit, but the roads dry off quickly. So, with time on my hands, I got into road-biking a bit more seriously. On the road, the falls are less frequent; but, if shit happens, it happens at three times the speed and the landings are a whole lot harder.

I had bought a beautiful Italian road-bike a few years previously – just to look at really. It is a classic steel Pinarello, in the white-and-pink colours of Jan Ullrich's 'controversial' T-Mobile squad. It reminds me of the bikes used by the inscrutable Miguel Indurain to win the Tour de France umpteen times, although clearly it has a much smaller 'engine'. Indurain, we may note, is still a 'free man'.

During the autumn of 1998, awaiting the arrival of the 'miracle baby', I usually managed to get out for two or three hours a day. I must have racked up about 1,500 kilometres during the autumn on the endless, winding lanes of Hampshire, plus another 500km on the mountain-bike, squeezed in during a flying visit to Scotland.

The final bike-ride, before we brought Samuel home to Jakarta, was magic. The soft glow of a low winter sun flattered the modest contours of the South Downs. It was unseasonably warm for New Year: up around 14 or 15 degrees, but windy; stuff of memories.

From the Western Approaches, a winter gale battered the South Coast. It took me a little while to get the hang of cranking the bike over to windward, to counter gusts of up to 50kts exploding through gaps in the hedgerows. The windsurfing experience helps, but only a little.

In conditions like these, even the 5cm side profile of the little Campagnolo aero-profiled rims proved to be something of a liability, as the bike revealed an alarming facility to rocket sideways at warp speed.

But I eventually got the hang of most of the roadie stuff – changing gears without losing too many of them and counter-steer the corners without grinding the pedals. However, the challenges of stopping never went away. Now, twenty years later, the stopping issue has been solved with the new generation of chunky road-bikes.

Fatter tyres and disk brakes make a huge difference, not just to stopping, but also to handling and safety on England's rapidly disintegrating road pavements. But, as I am now 'old school', my road-bikes still are too. I have to pick my way between the potholes like a figure-skater; maybe a 'gravel bike' is on the cards for next winter? (a cyclocross bike has indeed now joined the stable)

Meanwhile, out on the roads of Hampshire I see more and more blank expressions among the new legions of 'black riders' – a species sporting matching shoes and socks and exclusivity-priced Rapha-chic. Other, less-cool, weekend-warriors test the limits of Lycra stretch with replica team kit.

And, sometimes these days, I even see road-bikes with three chainrings and occasionally just one. Heaven forbid!

A chorus-line of starfish

1999, Lombok: The hidden hazard attending a measure of sporting achievement in one's youth is that our forties become a decade of desperation, awaiting the onset of decrepitude and decay. The more lightly you wear the self-confidence that comes with even modest competitive success at some remote point in your dim-and-distant past, the more leaden is the inexorable onset of physical self-doubt.

This hit me tonight, as I came down from the most enervating 'running high' that I can remember for ages. Rough running has always been a favourite recreation. Driving wind-powered vessels round arbitrary co-ordinates was always too serious a business for me to derive much enjoyment from it.

What hit me was: at 47 years of age, I can still do more-or-less everything I ever could, including, and perhaps even more so than anything else, running up hills. So, what happens when you do finally grow old? It must come pretty, bloody suddenly, since I can't see myself doing this at 67............ or 57?

But when your knees are gone, there's always cycling – favoured recreation of septuagenarians in denial. Last weekend in Jakarta, I picked up an extra set of narrow rims fitted with road slicks; easier than bringing two bikes here. So, after lunch on Saturday, I set out on a road-ride along the black-top lanes south of Mount Rinjani.

The change of tyres transforms the mountain-bike-on-the-road experience – it's quiet and progress becomes more efficient.

However, as with out-and-back rides on a proper road-bike, that level of efficiency means it's an awful long way home when you finally peg out at the furthest point. I compounded the felony by rattling on past my hotel and up to the Senggigi strip for a big beer and a large plate of chilli con carne.

You can also go off-road with slicks and, with the smaller rolling diameter you gain few more inches of gearing, so big hills are no problem, if it's hardpack. Coming down, I discovered, is another matter. So, on Sunday, I put the fat-tyres back on and climbed some more hills.

The southern foothills of Mount Rinjani resemble nothing so much as a chorus-line of starfish, ignoring for the moment the small matter of scale. Steep narrow ridges, with deeply incised intervening valleys, buttress the lower slopes of the mountain. There is always at least one trail up every valley and another down each ridge.

The fun part of this is that, to return to the asteroidean analogy for a moment, when you get to the starfish's armpit it gets seriously steep and technical; similarly, when going down, it starts to get exciting around the Brobdingnagian Asteroidea's second knuckle.

Once you are on the fingernails, 'front-pointing' comes into its own – a makeshift descending technique that takes advantage of the fact you don't have to pedal down a cliff, so you can dig in the raised slope-side crank, which becomes a crampon, and 'weight' the outside pedal. It's safer than it sounds and works well, as long as you always fall off towards the hill.

This year I am 68 – everything and nothing has changed.

Dog-day afternoons

1999, Lombok: On big international development projects, sectoral specialists come and go. As a project manager, in residence for the duration, sometimes I had excellent company and sometimes I didn't. During one stint in Lombok, we assembled a group of fit and enthusiastic fell-runners. This brought the reciprocal joys of company and competition to my evening runs.

Inevitably, we planned to climb Mount Rinjani. At 3,726 metres, and rising from sea-level, the volcano dominates the island. We made plans and assembled an experienced, well-equipped party. The team made a fast ascent without problems and had a great time. As luck would have it, I spent that long-weekend in a hospital bed in Singapore.

At the risk, no, let's be honest, the absolute certainty, of straying into half-assed, amateur philosophy, here goes. Life: I have some hypotheses about that. First, however, the essential background, or at least as much as you need.

The 'Chaos Theory' absolves weathermen and structural engineers world-wide of any responsibility to advise home-owners that roofs must be fixed down as well as propped up. They do this by reference to a butterfly in the Amazon jungle and the maxim – 'well bugger me, seasonal weather again this year'.

Since a strong enough breeze, blowing over any sort of a hump-shaped building-bump, will create enough negative pressure to hoist a garden-shed into the sky, that indifference

gives me the essential empirical underpinnings I need to define the related theory of: 'Shit happens, happens frequently, and often during my weekends off'.

Nothing we do in life is without significance. Each action, or indeed inaction, contributes in some way to the subsequent course of our lives. There are no safe options. Thus, if a life's course could be viewed as a tangible continuum, it would consist of a dense stream of storylines, interwoven with a tangled mesh of feed-back loops. Some of these loops would be made of barbed wire; well, at least mine would.

The practical result of life's essential characteristic of dredging-up things-past, to see whether they can be recycled in the future, is that every now and then, just when you least expect it, knotted lifelines duck back behind you and give you a well-placed kick in the ass. Well, that's exactly what happened to me.

I began to ride regularly, and with a new spirit of resolution, during rehab following an ACL reconstruction in 1994. This rekindled interest in cycling also served to ameliorate withdrawal symptoms from boardsailing and squash.

Last Saturday, all the hard work invested, to build over-size thigh muscles to support my weakened knees, came back to haunt me. These mutant muscles have just ripped apart the largest bone in my body.

Kampung Gunung Sari: It is a glorious afternoon; I am spinning effortlessly downhill on a well-graded backroad, buoyed up with anticipation of a couple of hours of brisk exercise in the hills. The way is clear. I am probably travelling at less than 40kph. I am set four-square for a sucker-punch.

Everything changes in an instant. Suddenly, a dog materialises in front of me. My front wheel smashes into the animal's ribcage and, simultaneously, I am flying – staying aloft long enough to: compare the dog to a bag of cement; to

experience an all-too-brief moment of exhilaration as I perform a slow roll to starboard; and to inexplicably encounter a (very short) rush of relief that this will not be so bad after all.

I bounce once in a neat five-point landing. I can feel my helmet absorbing the shock and note with momentary satisfaction that this one seems to work quite well. I glance up and see the bike sailing over my head to skate off down the road on its own.

A crowd forms instantaneously, surrounding me in a thicket of skinny brown legs. The guys respect my request for a few moments stock-taking-time, as I run through my standard damage check procedures. Pretty much everything hurts like hell, but nothing seems to be too radically displaced.

The good people of Gunung Sari carry me with unexpected tenderness into a nearby teahouse and set me out on the red felt dais like an embalmed Lenin. The resources of the village are mobilised. The local orang pijat (masseur, faith healer) cleans out my road-rash and checks for broken bones.

I am served hot, sweet coffee. Someone brings my gear and places thoughtfully it in my field of vision. Someone else repairs my sunglasses. They are concerned about concussion. A student visiting his family arrives to translate, but we get along fine in Bahasa, delighting the onlookers. "They seldom get to look at a Bule, close-up like this, Pak."

Sometime later, my new friends decide I am fit to make the trip back to the hotel. The coffee is already 'paid for' and there is no charge for the first aid. With some difficulty, I am placed on the pillion of the student's Suzuki 125. The orang pijat follows along behind on my bicycle. He is a little guy, and they have no Allen-keys, so he is obliged to ride on the crossbar.

The 'medevac' experience: I am blown away by the logistics. Tuesday morning, back in Jakarta, this huge ambulance arrives

to pick me up. I have a doctor with a big black bag to accompany me, all the way to my hospital bed in Singapore. I also have a nurse. There are drivers; there are 2 or 3 reps at the airport; there is another ambulance in Singapore, more reps, more nurses.

More than a dozen people to get me there (though, as it turns out later, no one to get me back). Flying from Lombok to Jakarta, before an authorised doctor ticked the boxes for my insurance company, I just hopped up the stairway onto the plane. Although, to be honest, that rash attempt at self-sufficiency didn't turn out to be great idea.

Singapore: I pride myself on my Singlish; I speak it like a native. It's a completely free-form abrogation of the sacred English language. It is so expressive; I just love it. *"Eh George, you just like the Kennedy, ah, got a lot of thing happen you, got the 'Brave Jean', lah"*.

This tangential observation invokes a tubby little fishing boat out of the port of Buckie in Fife. Only later, did I discover that the papers had been full of the latest capers of the testosterone-fuelled Kennedy family of Massachusetts and the so-called 'risk-taking gene'.

Now I have a big stainless-steel butterfly in my right hip. "Ayagh, got something metal sharp in there, lah", as my nurse said of the post-op X-ray. The 'open reduction and tension band wiring of the greater trochanter' brings me reluctantly into the body piercing 1990s.

And that's it, six weeks for the bones to knit and another six weeks before I can run up the hill at Senggigi.

The breeze is the fourth dimension

1999, Lombok: This is for Kathryn: The late Ricki Fulton, in his incomparable persona of the Reverend I. M. Jolly, used to gently ridicule the home-spun philosophy of 'Late Call' (Scottish Television's late lamented 'Thought for the Day'). "Life is like an ashtray, full of wee butts." Anything pretentious tickled his dog-collar. Ergo – follows a dog-collar tickled.

Consider this: The breeze is the fourth dimension. A balmy, still afternoon in the tropics – blue sky, blue sea and a big orange sun beating mercilessly down.... What's missing?

Rerun the tape.

This time, by mid-morning, the warm breath of a land breeze engraves a light texture on the surface of the ocean and introduces the merest hint of motion in the palm canopy. This time, by mid-day, the sea is every shade of blue and flecked with white; the coconut trees are in constant motion; Balinese blade banners yield to the gusts – fluttering, snapping nervously. Sitting on the beach, we can feel the air we breathe. Dormant senses come alive. The world stirs. The day is animated.

The onshore breeze, perhaps more so than all the other winds of the world, ignites something buried deep in our primeval psyche. On occasion, this can be a real buzz. A deep-seated stomach cramp of almost sensual well-being spreads up through the chest, tightening and constricting our breath, before rushing into the temples as an overwhelming feeling of euphoria.

On glorious days such as these, my restricted mobility nourishes alternative perspectives. For the moment, I cannot rip sensation from all-consuming physical activity. But I find the sensitivity of my deeply buried passive receptors markedly heightened. I am drunk with harmless good spirits when the wind blows.

I talk to everyone I meet, and everyone gives me freely of their time. (They do not know the frivolous manner of my disability. Ha!) Wielding crutches renders you harmless. If you are ever lonely, get a set. I have been reduced to crutches many times now, so at least I have good ones. I am also fairly skilled in their operation. Ergo, life is not so bad.

Today was Indonesian National Day and thus a public holiday. The weather was perfect, as it has been almost every day since I arrived here, exactly four months ago, on the 21st of April 1999. In Lombok, sunglasses are not a fashion accessory.

I drove over to Gunung Sari to revisit 'the scene of the crime' and thank the family who saw their front garden turned into circus three weeks ago. The best china was produced, and the old red baize was rolled out again. As I relaxed in good company, I began to appreciate that I was probably going much too fast down that narrow little road.

Since my personal development ground to a gentle halt a few years ago, I have grubbed around disconsolately for any cumulative gains which may still be on offer. In terms of the basic capability of the machine (and 'the ghost' in it, with apologies to Locke), decline and decay are now defining characteristics.

In rehab, of course, things are different: Each day is filled with surprise and delight as I discover things I couldn't do yesterday. I am setting targets and generally meeting them, physically at any rate. I have an odd feeling that I may now be repeating myself. Now, where was I?

For some reason, which remains an enigma to me, these gains are largely made during the tedious insomnia of the wee small hours. I need exercise to sleep. Thus, every morning, when I slide out of bed and pre-flight the body, it is with a little less discomfort. This continual improvement has sown the germ of a completely mad idea in my addled consciousness.

By decontextualizing the recovery, and decoupling it from my old exercise regime, I plan to motor through my prior benchmarks and overshoot. Then I can seize back one or two of the faculties I have lost through carelessness over the past few years.

I am thinking in particular of squash and windsurfing and keeping up with Alan on the road bike. Getting about is getting easier. Although, if I can be brutally frank here, my adrenaline count for the month is still unlikely to hit double figures.

Wind of passage. Image - the Author

Swiss rolls

1999, Lombok: It's been a couple of months. Today, for the first time since my enforced medical time-out in Singapore, I pulled the bike out of its hibernation in the hotel storeroom and set out on the island's highways and byways. I cycled past the scene of 'the accident' and climbed a few hills to overprint my bad memories with some good ones.

I topped out a moderate climb, where the dirt road changed to a rocky track, beside a big stack of timber. On average, these logs were 3 metres long and 30 centimetres in diameter. At the risk of revelling in a cliché, I witnessed another remarkable women-carrying-stuff-on-heads feat.

A young girl walked down the hill past me and, without apparent effort, dumped another huge tree-trunk on the growing stack; then she set off back up the hill for another one. I could lift one end with one hand, but only just. That's why, with a five-gallon drum of water on their heads, the girls are happy to stand and chat at the well.

Meanwhile the gentlemen of the household sit on the terrace and toke on foul-smelling kretek cigarettes. Even if they were inclined to work the land, there is not much left. The kids have persuaded their grandparents to exchange the eternal gift of heritable padi fields for the transient happiness of a shiny new Japanese motorbike.

Even more insidious, is another trend. Selfish, polygamous patriarchs sell-up to save their soul. The money they receive

finances a Haj pilgrimage to Mecca. The newly elevated hajis return destitute, having squandered the timeless assets that supported their families for generations.

The next day, I changed wheels and cycled up the coast to the little port of Bangsal where the boats leave for the Gilli islands. This is a fine road, made up of short flat stretches which detour behind picture-postcard catenary beaches of pale-golden sands. The easy sections are interrupted by testing climbs over the headlands and fast descents down them. The roads are so steep here that you have to wedge the nose of the saddle into your bottom to keep the front wheel on the ground.

The hot air warps and wobbles as it rises from the melting asphalt. The surface is cracked like crazy paving and I imagine that someday the asphalt wearing-course will detach from the roads base-course and Swiss-roll me back down the hill, like the jam filling in a retracting kazoo trumpet.

I doubled back at the harbour 30kms out and returned to the coast to confront a brisk 25kt sou'wester with watery knees. And, of course, that was another case of an ordinary, everyday excursion turning into a desperate struggle to outpace the shadow the setting sun as it raced to meet the far horizon.

Getting home options, Senggigi Beach, Lombok. Image - the Author

Groundhog Day

1999, Lombok: The film 'Groundhog Day' comes to mind. I remember something similar last year. I had a big wreck that resulted in a few days 'down time' in hospital, reflecting on how much longer things take to heal at our age, and how a small error in judgement can exact a disproportionate penalty. My biking-buddy had called off that day, so I was alone. And, when I go out on my own, things seldom go according to plan.

After a good hard three-hour ride, I was tired and careless. I cleared a small drop-off and found some newly dug steps on the downslope; but I took it much too slowly. In these situations, everyone knows that speed is your best friend; caution is not just ill-advised it's reckless.

Unsurprisingly, the front wheel stopped, and the back wheel didn't, so I sailed clear over the bars and landed a few metres further down this seemingly benign little hill.

Well, I landed equally in my head and two hands: a classic face-plant. I thought I had broken both wrists, but fortunately only one – as it transpired, the more painful of the two was just sprained.

More interesting was what had happened to my head, still strapped securely into its helmet, but now rattling a bit. I had never experienced concussion before. I had no idea it was like this: As I sat up my vision dissolved in an orange 'white-out'. Slowly, that cleared to reveal a golden landscape shape-shifting eerily through a misty curtain of falling snow.

I set off through this strange blizzard, leaning against the bike for support, with my elbows covered in red mud and probably singing 'Auntie Leezie's Current Bun'.

Fortunately, when I had the accident, I had already returned to within a kilometre or so of the trailhead, after being perhaps 20 kilometres distant earlier in the loop. Some indeterminate time later, having zigzagged drunkenly across the padi fields, I staggered into the local café where I'd parked the car.

With great good fortune, I ran into an old friend there. Peter was laying a run for the Jakarta Hash House Harriers and had stopped by for a beer and a curry. We had a good laugh at my predicament. I euphorically hosed myself down as best I could and locked the bike in the back of the Kijang.

At this point, my recollection of events gets a bit hazy as my self-preservation instincts cut out. I crawled into Peter's car and lay down feeling violently sick; then I lost my vision again. This time I entered 'warp drive' – everything was blinding white and rushing towards me; and this time, I thought it might just be permanent.

We had an alarming ride into town. I could hear angry horns and squealing tyres. All the while, I implored Peter to weigh the benefits of killing us both, against me arriving at the emergency department a few minutes earlier.

When we finally got there, the blizzard was clearing, still with light snow and interference and still in black and white, but at least I could see. After a childhood enduring the awful TV reception in the Scottish Highlands, I thought I could handle that; and so we stumbled into the Intensive Care Unit and unadulterated relief.

I was so happy; I was quite unprepared for Alison's reaction to finding me connected-up to a big vital signs machine, auto-drip device, neck-collar, one plastered wrist to the elbow, one in a big bandage and little cuts and bruises and iodine splashes all over the place.

At this point, my dear friend was seven months pregnant and due to return to Britain in a few days. Understandably, perhaps, she was not amused.

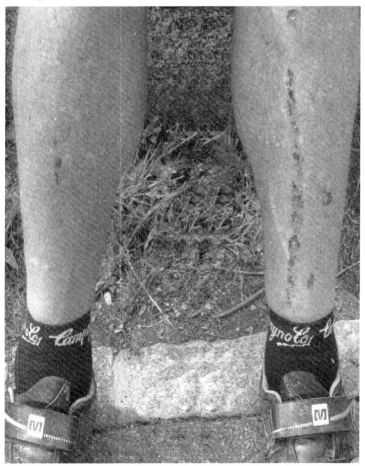

A not atypical day on the bike.   Image - the Author

Sasak circumcision parties

1999, Lombok: The World Bank Review Mission is scheduled to visit soon and doubtless entrain more mayhem. The big development banks are not content lending money; they have made meddling an art-form. After nine months of indecision, for the remaining three months of our programme, we will be obliged to rebrand everything once again.

As from now, the team will proudly march under the gloriously irresolute banner of the 'Lombok Poverty Alleviation and Environmental Infrastructure Project'. Some infinitives are just asking to be split.

As a marching band, however, we leave much to be desired; we have yet to achieve the type of intoxicating rhythms that make Sasak circumcision parties such a great day out. Out by Jerringo, on a fine technical trail, I stumbled across one such circumcision. An elaborate procession wound its way up the path as I came down. I pulled over to enjoy the spectacle.

First to pass were the kids and hangers-on, driven before the party by a bulldozer section of enormous base drums. These drums are slung horizontally, but are almost two metres deep, so that unless you are an orang-utan, you can only bang on one side. Then family and friends, dressed in batik and shiny black linen, tailored in the local style, sauntered through; elegant and very sharp.

Amid this merry throng, two small boys crouched in an upholstered sedan chair, grimly clutching a symbolic yellow brolly. I glimpsed worried little faces, squinting through beads of sweat and a pancake of traditional makeup.

Toddlers-in-trouble, hoisted aloft in the bosom of a happy family, wracked by second thoughts. Someone must have let on what was about to happen to a couple of near and dear members. An incisive percussion section brought up the rear, blocking the obvious escape route.

Male genital mutilation: a blunt instrument in the field of personal hygiene, in a land where cutting-edge technology is performed with a rusty knife.

Sedan chair litter, Borobudur, Java. Image - the Author

The music of chance

1999, Lombok: Out on the bike one day, I joined Alice on the far side of the Looking Glass. We came upon a bizarre marching band. It was brilliant; we tagged along for ages, with my imaginary friend sustaining my state of suspended disbelief through her customary witty commentary.

A new, and possibly unique, folk music tradition has developed on the island since it first emerged, blinking into the light of day in the 1970s. It is very Brazilian, and a perhaps a little bit Ska. Something like forty assorted drummers, hammering maniacally, lay down layers of hard-edged rhythmic noise.

Over the top of this inspired cacophony, raucously amplified keyboards, fingered in the dangduk-style of the Indian sub-continent, scythe from the bundled bullhorns of half-a-dozen old public-address systems.

The keyboard players ride in style on dogcart-like chariots; perched atop banks of old car batteries. They are propelled by clusters of willing volunteers; there are no rickshaws on Lombok. The drummers simply walk, staggering stoically on foot under their burden, adding arbitrary half-beats and elements of random syncopated colour.

Afterwards, back at the beach, I met a German musicologist called Gunter. This enthusiastic gentleman had been conducting folk-music research in Bali, returning every year for more than a decade now. He obviously has the sort of generous paid-holiday that is much reviled by free-marketeers on our side of the English Channel.

But, researching gamelan music, really? Gamelan is right up there with Javanese opera as an exercise in mind-numbing, perhaps even mind-controlling, entertainment. Only traditional communities with no petrol for the generator and infinite time on their hands could conjure that stuff up.

I set him straight on that one and brought his attention to Lombok's indigenous music scene, which he has somehow missed for a decade. Obviously, I need to introduce him to my imaginary friend Alice.

What I love about all this, is that they are building a grassroots tradition that owes nothing to their other side-line of tourist-tattle 'gongathons' or the global pandemic of MTV.

The village of Aikmel is the place, apparently. I intend to go there one Sunday with the old Walkman Professional and capture some of this magic on tape.

Kids on Senggigi Beach, Lombok. Image - the Author

The big dipper

1999, Lombok: Saturday afternoon, to loosen things up after a week of long and not-very-productive hours in the office, I rattled the 60 klicks up and down the big-dipper coast-road on the mountain-bike. Twenty years later, I am still nostalgic about the sensory pleasures of cycling gallusly through the hot breeze of the tropics, slicing solid air.

On my return, I promptly fell asleep exhausted until about 9.30 p.m. and missed the all-important sunset ritual on the beach. No hot sand, no cold beer, alas, and no big plastic bottle of Coke and sweets for the village kids either.

Not such a loss in the wet-season, although the evenings are still pretty-enough, in countless shades of grey and pale custard, with a spacious and slightly unsettling three-dimensionality introduced by the clear air and the, seemingly further, far horizon.

The following morning, I put the fat tyres back on the bike and set off for Mambalan – more familiar to me as good running country with the Lombok Hash House Harriers. I lucked into some subliminal single-track beyond a hill-top warung where, on a previous occasion, I bought the local kids a great bundle of fruit-flavoured ice-sticks, enjoyed the celebrity of the moment, and then turned back.

I contoured round behind the same hill, somewhat precariously on the more exposed sections, to arrive in a concealed valley of terraced waterfalls in full flood. It was a

transcendently gloopy and slithery landscape that should surely have slumped to earth years ago. God knows where all this water was coming from.

Dank green cliffs rose uninterrupted on three sides. The valley was off the beaten track; no sweetie-papers or cigarette packets. The only damper on this mini-wilderness-experience was the lack of an obvious way out, bar a resolution-sapping scramble up 200 metres of near-vertical soggy hillside to an assumed ridge-top trail.

It took me about an hour, and I suppose it was a minor epic. It's clear that fatigue has set in when it seems like a good idea to sling the bike up the hill above you, and then use it to pull yourself up afterwards. Of course, what happens is that the uncooperative machine slides right back down on top of you, along with half a cubic metre of mud and slimy groundcover. And, for sure you are wasted, when you do this more than once.

As a small bonus, inductive logic worked and there was indeed a fine trail on the ridge, albeit hidden beyond about three false summits. The real hilltop revealed a generous vista of the whole of Central Lombok and three extremely fit, and rather smug-looking, cows.

I was tempted for a while to carry on up, but exhaustion and the gathering dusk suggested that I bail out. I doubled back to a recognisable junction with trodden-path villager's path and went for the big downhill. That was even less fun; my shin muscles were in spasms and my arches knotted with cramp.

It was sheer hell. It was another great Lombok bike ride.

Twenty years later, I am still nostalgic about the sensory pleasures of cycling gallusly through the hot breeze of the tropics, slicing solid air.

There's a shark in my beer

1999, Lombok: I had picked up some virulent bug and was forced to spent most of Saturday laid-up in bed, ignoring the raucous screams and laughter of happy Dutch families baking bodies around the pool and generally having a good time. However, I did make an effort to get out on the bike for a few hours on the Saturday afternoon.

About eight kilometres from the hotel, a neatly manicured vale of lush rice terraces runs deep into the foothills before dividing into two increasingly steep and wooded valleys. I am sure it is possible to traverse the watershed ridge between the headwaters of these two gullies and complete the loop but so far, I have failed miserably. They could be miles apart, or as I suspect, just a hill away. So, for the moment it's two one-way rides.

The upper reaches of both valleys are equally entrancing. This is a man-made landscape consummated over generations. An intricate trellis of sandy trails is shaded by a lofty dappled canopy, pierced by slivers of golden sunlight. It is a very special place. These are pathways to linger over and to savour, rather than bash through, head down and breathless.

Fleeting rites of passage enfold the smell of damp leaves crushed under the tyres. The soft chatter of running water coursing between rounded river rocks melds with the constant babble of a million unseen insects. The trail emerges into an open grassy knoll and subliminal views to the outside world are momentarily revealed. These jungle rides invoke in me the

warm and fuzzy ambience of a stroll along the country lanes of Devon on a rare hot summer's day.

Up above the 250 metre contour circumstances change abruptly. Grey rain-clouds envelope the head of the valley. I sat down on a large rock and watched outstretched palm fronds squirm under the deluge, while the jungle shivered, and the trail became a muddy torrent. Time to retire to the pub?

There is a bar a kilometre down the road from the Jayakarta Hotel called the Shark Club. It's a strange place. I first noticed it when they showed the Rugby World Cup on TV. 'Klub Hiu' is run as a hobby pub by an ex-B-movie actor, now in business on the island. It seems he just wants to enjoy a quiet game of pool in clean and bright surroundings. I have seen one of David's movies; he is a brave man indeed to ham it up in his own pub.

Klub Hiu is seldom busy; it is off the tourist track. Thus, the elegant English-speaking staff always make a great fuss of me. The draft beer is not cheap, but it comes equipped with a little shark carved out of bone swimming round the bottom of the glass. Maybe its shark bone and maybe it isn't.

Senggigi Beach, Lombok. Image - the Author

Slum-junkie

1999, Liaoning: I was unfamiliar with the slums of cold climates. In Shenyang, every miserable hovel is planned round a chimney, built as tall as salvaged materials will allow. Everything and anything combustible is slung up onto the roof of the shack over the summer months, in anticipation of the long hard winter. There is a broken table, a mattress, half a sideboard, logs-from-God-knows-where, old sofas and shattered scraps of shuttering joinery.

We passed an old man bludgeoning a big pile of this detritus into splinters with a ball-head hammer, to produce a week's supply of firewood. Nothing is wasted. I thought of buying him an axe, but that thought occurred to me only later that evening in the bar after dinner when the chances of finding this place again were zero.

In the slums, as indeed everywhere in 1990s China, bicycles were ubiquitous. I wondered how they would manage to get about in winter without falling over. I thought that an already hazardous activity would become infinitely more so. Later, I would discover the sanctuary of the journey-to-work peloton and the magic of safety in numbers.

On the way home, we came across the most impressive bicycle-powered food stall I have seen throughout the length and breadth of Asia. This contrivance, larger than some adjacent dwellings, was abandoned on the corner of an alley. It seems that Manchuria's 'Desperate Dan' expired in the saddle at that point and, since then, no one has been able to move his restaurant trike.

Later that afternoon, I went out for a run to take advantage of the relatively clean air which floods the city when the smelter is shut down on high days and holidays. The first-and-last-jogger-in-Shenyang prompted a few dozy cyclists to bolt, but otherwise generated very little wake. Unless you run round-and-round the block, jogging in any city is constantly interrupted by junctions, road crossings and red lights. Nothing looks as daft as running on the spot, apart from attempting a track-stand on the bike.

My natural gait is a little above the local pedalling pace, so it was marginally less risky than I anticipated. However, it did confirm that I couldn't cycle here myself through the stop-go streets for any kind of a decent workout; unless, perhaps, I was pushing Dan's tricycle restaurant in front of me.

Shortly afterwards, of course, I bought a bike and discovered the network of dirt roads and canal-side tracks that lie just beyond the concrete, steel and glass of the city centre; and I found plenty of open road upon which to exhaust myself.

Shortly afterwards, of course, I bought a bicycle and discovered the network of dirt roads and canal-side tracks that lie just beyond the concrete, steel and glass of the modern city centre; and I found plenty of open road and a labyrinth of fascinating alleys and backstreets to explore.

Today, we bought a bicycle

2000, Liaoning: Today we bought a bicycle. Right now, I have 8.5 bicycles, not counting the ones I bought for other members of the family, which I am still obliged to keep clean and generally look after. The new bike is a miracle of 'cheap transportation'; just how cheap it was will shortly become apparent.

Since our remaining inputs will not overlap, Don and I have bought the bike together. You have no idea how that throws people here. 'Our bike' is a contradiction in terms. It's like sharing underpants.

We went to 'bicycle alley', not too far from the project office. Out counterpart, Hong Kai, closed the deal on a glossy, silver-grey 'Firebird'. It's a neatly assembled, single-speed hybrid, with nice geometry, if a little long in the chainstays. But, alas, this Firebird was forged in a bonfire, not a furnace.

It's an unassuming ode to mild steel; about as stiff as Playdoh and similarly bereft of life. I'd estimate that it tips the scales at about 65lbs, or the weight of my Look and Pinarello road-bikes, plus my old dual-suspension Cannondale thrown-in to level the hypothetical balance-bar.

With an extra-long seat-post, a wheel lock and half the shop's ring spanners to tune it up, we finally paid Y310. That's around eleven quid each. This evening, Don and went out for a meal and few beers and spent about same amount of money. I'm still not sure which was better value.

The Chinese find the long seat-post hilarious. Propped against a wall, the freak-show bike immediately attracts a crowd. They are mystified as to why anyone would want to sit so high up. Riding it, we enjoy the status of circus performers. Everyone here sets the saddle just above the top-tube and pedals with their heels, legs akimbo. It looks excruciating.

Then there is registration. Agents do this for you on the street. They are everywhere. However, we went from one to another until we had strayed so far from the office that we had to take a taxi back. Everyone, it seems, had run out of tags; it was Saturday afternoon.

Registration is 50p. Fitting the plate, stamping the number on the seat tube and laminating the license are all free. And we got to choose an auspicious number. It seems there have been 2,305,937 bicycles caught and tagged here. And yet, Don spotted No.46 on the way home – way cool.

The plates are elaborate. The centre section slides out as a key fob. If you can complete the jigsaw puzzle, and the number on the frame matches the plate, it's clearly your bike – an ingenious challenge, and fun in itself on a wet day.

It's a system that works so well, Hong Kai lost only two bikes last year. Hopefully, we will have the Firebird long enough to register it another couple of times and take-home souvenir numberplates.

The Labour Day holiday starts tomorrow. Tang Ke reckoned we needed an extra bicycle for this, so I have borrowed his 'Long March' faux-mountain-bike. We all rode home in company. Hong Kai takes his role as 'minder' very seriously. Now, however, we are entirely on our own. Don peddled to work in Hanoi for two years, so he is unfazed. I am less sanguine. No SPDs, no helmet, no brakes worth a damn, and above all, no quarter.

I toured the city for a little over four hours the next afternoon. It was warm; it was sunny; it was Labour Day. So, as can imagine, the more obvious family-outing-spots were busy. On to 'Plan B': There are landscaped cycle-tracks along the major drainage canals. They were also crowded, but passable. I took a few detours and experienced some of the most depressing urban wastelands I have seen for some time.

It was, therefore, pretty much all down-hill, but it was also, somehow, all down-wind. The down-hill part I can work out. The city is flat; you could play pool on it. Since floodplains rival the 'red-mud' as the topography-of-last-resort on mountain-bikes, the unfamiliar-flat, by comparison, seems to be down-hill. The down-wind, I can't explain.

After just one afternoon exploring the city without continually coming up against the language barriers that make taxi rides a nightmare, I reckon that the bike has returned my initial outlay.

Bike shop, Shenyang, China. Image - the Author

65

Sidewalk bicycle repair, Shenyang, China. Image - the Author

66

Sidewalk bicycle repair, Shenyang, China. Image - the Author

Three friendly North Koreans

1999, Liaoning: The air continues to clear across north-east China. On the second day of the public holiday, the horizon has receded beneath a leaden overcast sky. To the north-east, I can now see distant mountains. Later, it cleared up and the sun came out, but the temperature for the day dipped to 2 degrees and in the brisk north-easterly it certainly felt like it.

Ian and I were trapped in the Holiday Inn's incongruous Irish Bar until well past bedtime by a three friendly North Koreans. The denizens of the DPRK regaled us with fascinating anecdotes in Russian. Well, we think it was Russian.

Sunday morning, and it's back to sunshine again. After a late breakfast, Michael, Martin and I explored the old city-block to the immediate south of the hotel; a low-rise island-slum in Shenyang's 'Brave New World'; an anthill with a million abandoned bicycles oxidising peacefully on the rooftops.

Few of these fascinating urban villages will survive the current development plan and, objectively, it's difficult to argue with that. However, in this case, urban renewal will destroy a community of obvious vitality and cohesion.

The district started life as planned workers' housing in the thirties. Today, the single-skin brick hovels lie buried beneath great mounds of hopeful recycling. Cluttered alleyways trace the remembered line of once-desirable urban streets and shady pavements. Yesterday's genteel main drag now hosts the worthless wall-to-wall commerce of a marginalised society in near-destitution.

Dead and dying plane-trees rise above the chaos to pierce the encroaching carpet of sidewalk shanties. Some of the stalls are little rusting steel boxes – series-produced retail units from some long-forgotten programme, perhaps? They must be desperately cold in winter.

Our self-appointed guide, a rotund one-eyed dwarf, points with demented enthusiasm – at more or less everything. Leering Mongols tend great wriggling mounds of enormously fat grubs steaming away on gas hobs. Aloof Moslems sell goat sate from the greasy dais of flat-bed business bicycles.

In the odd clear space, old-folks play cards on an upturned bucket; a little girl plays a skipping game with only a bent-wood chair to partner her. Michael takes their picture. I need my camera. I need to capture this stuff before it disappears.

Today, it has indeed all disappeared.

Quiet backstreet, Shenyang, China. Image - the Author

Plumes of sulphur dioxide

2000, Liaoning: Everyone should ride a bike in China, if only once. Cycling through the hidden districts of Shenyang I came across an intriguing time-warp of grey middle-class apartments and depressing brown tenements. These decaying buildings reminded me of the Glasgow slums demolished in 'comprehensive redevelopment schemes', back in the days before refurbishment became fashionable.

They were built by the Japanese during their annexation of Manchuria in the 1930s. The occupying forces and dirt-poor colonists thought they would be in Manchuoko for ever. The citizens of the 'Greater East Asia Co-Prosperity Sphere' did not anticipate Enola Gay.

Generally, however, the city north of the railroad, dynamited in the famous 'Mukden incident', is an endless urban wasteland of deadly Soviet-pattern eight-story walk-up blocks, linked to coal-fired district-heating plants, with towering brick smokestacks.

But there is more to see than old buildings. The traffic police in Shenyang are clearly an elite; uniquely in China, their uniforms fit properly. For my money, they outclass the chorus boys at Manilla's chaotic junctions, and even the balletic traffic cops of Bangkok. The basic style is robotic, the level of rigour – Marcel Marceau at his prime. It's pure theatre.

One of the major intersections here has an even more impressive figure on a box. Shenyang built one of the last big

Mao statues; it dominates Zhongshan Square. He stands imperious aloft, sensibly clad in well-cut greatcoat, pointing the way ahead, looking a bit like Indonesia's Suharto.

Round the base of the plinth, stony-faced red-guards and worker-ants in shallow base-relief brandish little red books. It's a wonderful piece of kitsch. It's huge. The cult of personality is still alive. At weekends, workers from the suburbs and star-struck out-of-towners cluster round to gaze reverentially aloft and have their photos taken in the shadow of the Great Helmsman.

From my 25th floor vantage point, on the roof of the hotel tonight, it was a Lowry out of Turner. The majesty of really tall chimneys pumping plumes of sulphur dioxide into a crosswind is undeniable and compounded when set against a brilliant, graduated backcloth of orange through beige and deep blue.

In the middle distance, the drab cityscape appeared as a uniform field of Stalinist apartments, edged in gold. And, through the entire depth of the scene, the petrified forest of domestic smokestacks was dramatically thrown into shadow. It's a powerful image, but hopefully not one which will shorten my life too much over the course of the project.

I thought the petrified forest might see out the decade, but every one of these magnificent chimneys has disappeared now.

Benxi, Liaoning, China. Image - the Author

Buying magazines, Xingcheng, China. Image - the Author

Red skies and red mud revisited

2000: It was a glorious spell in Jakarta. Strong winds whipped-up Dali-esque skies of the palest blue, striated with wispy little pink clouds, tinged with yellow – mad March hairs? At the weekends, Alison and I have cruised the furthest reaches of our extravagant pool, flopped atop lurid green loungers. We are sun-tanned like tourists, as is little Samuel, thwarting our best parenting efforts.

Time to revisit the telluric trails of Bojong? These past weeks, the heights of Gunung Putri (Princess Mountain) have loomed encouragingly over Cibubur, outlined in stark relief, under the vault of unusually clear air.

I had a loose arrangement to meet a group of local cyclists at the Boy Scout Camp but sailed on by; it just looked too good up in the hills. And it was – for a while. It was also, perhaps, too early in the season to commit to the mountain.

Just an hour into the ride, a malevolent charcoal smudge waddled over the ridgeline, gathered up its skirts and voided its engorged belly on the foothills. I was now placed strategically, stage-centre, in a 50-square kilometre tract of red mud. We have been here before. Suffice to say, getting out doesn't get any easier.

Back in Lombok for the working week, the sunset was again outstanding. The western sky was a translucent grey, mottled pink and shot with threads of gold. Bali was sharply defined as a glowing silhouette, revealing the full profile of that magical island.

I lived on the beach at Senggigi, on and off, for almost a year. I have observed the pacific sun as he swept the breadth of the western horizon. I witnessed his return from a summer solstice excursion to Nusa Penida, to retire behind Nusa Dua, dipping to rest after the long trek. Over the next few months, he would repeat the cycle and clamber back up to his rightful place, to roost awhile on the summit of Gunung Agung, before ranging north for more sea-time.

The moon also sets. The following morning: Cool-elegant-silver, she too lingered, poised, above Nusa Dua; then plunged helplessly to earth, resigned in distant bondage to her indifferent mentor, rising even now above the massive bulk of Gunung Rinjani, to open Tuesday in a gossamer haze of flamboyant orange.

Senggigi Beach – I love it.

Sunset over Bali from Senggigi Beach. Image - the Author

2nd Class seat-post

2000, Lombok: I was enjoying a great ride on the big top-loop above Jeringo, when I broke my seat-post. Split at the neck in two places. It was by far the lightest seat post I had – perhaps there is a connection there? The next act in the no-saddle scenario, where the stump is only interrupted by the top tube after a descent of 25cm, doesn't bear thinking about.

Nevertheless, the following day, I lashed it together with a yard of Kevlar string and followed the coast-road to Malimbu, to revisit a quite beautiful place.

One evening, some weeks before, I had been invited over to join a table of young local people. My solitary status can be fairly conspicuous at times, especially when I am maudlin. These guys were talking about buying some land that had been advertised for sale in Malimbu. It seems that they plan to develop a little community of native barflies.

My passing interest in the many manifestations of tropical island paradise roped me into providing transport the following day. They considered that I was unlikely to gazump them by offering a few more dollars a hectare.

From the best beach in Lombok (a beach known locally, perhaps inevitably, as 'Malibu') three kilometres of sump-scraping dry riverbeds and collapsing trails brought us, shaken and, yes, stirred too, to the doorstep of the land-in-question. It was located right at the trail-end and set in a breath-taking landscape of jungle-clad, knife-edge ridges interspersed with

75

neatly chomped buffalo meadows. I had now returned on the bike to explore.

There is a small dwelling in a cultivated clearing a kilometre or so from the road-end. My visit throws them a little. Still, I can see why I have brought the household's infants to tears. I remove my alien helmet, rehydration plumbing and Bono-shades. Then, I pass out small bills to the kids to make amends and introduce myself. Mea culpa, thus is the cult of 'minta uang' (money please), often erroneously interpreted as begging, perpetuated. The children are just as happy with a handful of sweets or a few minutes of conversation.

In these remote parts, where Europeans never go, my sudden appearance is a small miracle. Perhaps it triggers a flashback to the random, uncommon favours of Dutch Colonial times.

There are three boys and three girls. They are all less than ten years old and they are perhaps the most charming children I have ever come across, anywhere. I promised the family that I would return for afternoon tea, when I can arrange more daylight hours.

Back on the beach, the continuing sensational weather showcased local life. When we were kids in Kilmun, among our best friends, was a family who had spent time in Trinidad with Forest Department. There was a competent watercolour in pride of place, above the fireplace. This painting always fascinated me. It depicted 'the catch' being hauled in, hand-over-hand, by a line of native people in coolie hats.

For me, that was 'the tropics'. It still is. That afternoon, half a dozen teams of local villagers re-enacted the very same scene on Senggigi Beach.

Teamwork: Hauling big nets from the shore certainly epitomises the romantic ideal of cohesive, island fishing

communities; men, women, old, young, tiny children – all working together. Sadly, however, 500 linear metres of fine-mesh net may deliver no more than a small bucket of tiddlers.

And it's hard.

Yet, within the slowly shrinking perimeter of one huge net, the idyll of communal labour was dented a little by a cheeky maverick. This kid stood chest deep in the centre, defiantly fishing with a rod and line. It would have been bare-faced cheek, had the bandit not been hunched beneath a tall white Stetson and masked by a red, Deputy Dawg bandanna.

It made my day.

Cargo Cults still exist in this region, surviving the departure of Uncle Sam and the end of WW2. Some years ago, while carrying out fieldwork for a regional development project, I found the whole mysterious business alive and well in the Western Pacific – Biak Island and Irian Jaya, or rather now West Papua.

Hauling in the nets, Senggigi Beach, Indonesia. Image - the Author

The paper boy delivers the milk

2000, Lombok: In the first month of the new Millennium, the paradise island of Lombok was trashed by Islamic extremists. It was an event as unexpected as it was profane. A sleepy island community had been incited to rampage. For a time, riding bikes became less important, not to say unwise and maybe even lethal.

2.30 p.m. Monday: After a long night of destruction, the whole town cowered behind closed doors. Unsure how this would all pan out, we sat tight in the office, ringing round and listening to the radio, trying to find out what the hell was happening. Then we received a phone-call that the mob had unexpectedly regrouped. They were now looting shops a few miles away in Ampenan.

This created an escape window. So Selamat, our Office Manager, drove Greg and I back to the hotel. Pranoto, the Financial Analyst, came along to ride shotgun. The streets were tense and deserted, strewn with debris. We passed a truckload of Ninja-turtle police going in the opposite direction from the columns of smoke.

4.00 p.m. Monday: The hotel management are monitoring the police frequency. There are choppers patrolling overhead. It seems that Lombok's abashed security forces have decided to guard the tourists rather than confront the looters. For the moment, I won't argue with that. The hotel busses are still trapped at the airport.

10.30 p.m. Monday: Cordoned-off from the chaos, we had G&Ts on the beach and watched the columns of smoke rise over Ampenan. There was a big fire about a kilometre away, more-or-less where the Shark Club is. I hope not. Acrid smoke is drifting over the hotel grounds.

At last, we are on CNN: "*Eyewitness reports…. On the holiday island of Lombok, a mob etc….*" But no film and they know less than we do, bunkered here in the hotel.

Selamat has asked us to sit tight. It seems that the police have advised all foreigners to 'eat in' tonight. We had dinner in the unusually crowded pizza restaurant with Alan, an engaging American tourist from Boulder, Colorado.

While the mob roamed-at-large earlier today, our blithe 'innocent abroad' unknowingly went into the airport and postponed his flight; he was having such a good time in Lombok. Alan is unlikely to postpone his flight again tomorrow.

We had a busy programme this week, with a workshop planned for tonight and visits from the Director of Urban Development and the automatons of the World Bank. Sod it. The office will remain closed.

7.00 a.m. Tuesday: During the night, the looting and arson continued unabated on the other side of the Senggigi barricade; with four more churches, dozens of homes, shops and vehicles put to the torch. Through the early morning the rioters petrol-bombed a catholic hospital, a clinic, a pharmacy, and the Lombok nurse's residences – that was just a few tens of metres from the home of Suryani who arranges tours and travel here at the hotel.

Scores of young thugs are now in a different hospital, with well-deserved gunshot wounds; one or two are in the morgue. Few tears are shed for these boys among the shell-shocked islanders.

Bernardo, a financial analyst, phoned from Philippines about an hour before that, asking whether or not he should get on the plane. I told him to stay put. Then at 6.00 a.m. this morning, I discussed the situation with the senior staff and decided to shut down the project for the meantime and evacuate.

Selamat arrived on a motorcycle, his Christianity 'disguised' under a haji skull-cap. He has gone off to beg, borrow, bribe or steal air-tickets. The plan is for us all to fly out today.

9.00 p.m. Tuesday: We set off for the airport at 10.30; early, before the mob shook off the hangover induced by their orgy of violence last night. The Hotel Manager led our small convoy on a high-speed ride through the almost deserted streets, past lazy wisps of smoke from last night's fires. The huddled masses camped out at the airport were almost exclusively middle-class Chinese. The sat there with blood-shot eyes, blank expressions, and a few pathetic possessions; persecuted yet again.

In the Executive Lounge, somehow open today for brazen economy class passengers, a special forces soldier with a large gun told us that the mob were in action about two kilometres away. Shortly afterwards, we saw three trucks packed with riot police head off in that direction. Then the crowd in the departure lounge observed a few minutes silence to watch their home-town burn on the lunchtime news.

After that, things began to look up. Alan shouted ice-cold beers with the change from the ten bucks I took to cover his departure tax. Then I scored a good swap with one of our central government colleagues. I exchanged my Bali flight for boarding cards to Jakarta via Surabaya. Where Ir. Nuriadi got the ticket, I don't know.

I flew back to Jakarta as 'Mr Kikki'; co-incidentally the name of the Regional Armed Forces Commander, chattering aloft in a Huey at that very moment. My new rank didn't secure me any special treatment, but I did get home. We reconvened the project team in Jakarta. I rented a house and we got on with the job.

I returned to the island some months later for a situation assessment. There was something surreal about dinner at the Sheraton that evening. Our party of twenty, a motley confederation of World Bank officers, senior government officials, local politicians and jobbing consultants, sat by the poolside at a long trestle-table. The food was good, and the service was excellent.

We were cosseted in splendid isolation. The only guests at the five-star resort hotel, save the Bank, were a conference of Sheraton's regional managers, dining elsewhere. For bargain-hunters, the walk-up room-rate is now $50. If you are not unsettled by the post-apocalypse ambience, it's a good deal.

Some months later, I was back in my more modest rooms at the Jayakarta, to collect my bike and trot around after another World Bank Mission. I arrived late on a Sunday afternoon with sufficient daylight to run up the hill behind the hotel. Somehow fittingly, it was a misty evening with a light drizzle.

However, I was warmly welcomed with the usual 'hellos' extended on this occasion to touching 'thank-yous', simply for running through their village. The island's abrupt plunge from poverty into destitution was evident on the trail. No fag packets and no sweetie papers.

A few restaurants reopened that week and presented a brave face, brightly lit yet empty. But others, among them the Shark Club, the Marina Pub and Ronaldo's Bar were open only to the sky.

The Shark Club was hit about half an hour before lunch on the third day of madness. Two boys rode by on a motorcycle with a satchel of Molatov cocktails. Like a paperboy delivering the milk, they barely slowed down to sling the fire-bomb, on their way to make further flying drops at other unsuspecting 'parlours of vice' along the road to Senggigi.

Outriggers, Senggigi Beach, Indonesia. Image - the Author

Watermarks

2000, Liaoning: Tonight, cycling through the streets of the old town, we saw the human spirit revealed with a flourish on the grimy sidewalk.

Old men, with beer bottles modified to write like great fat fountain pens, practised the fine art of calligraphy before an admiring crowd. They don't have the money for brushes, scrolls and ink, but water costs them nothing. So, a soggy carpet of innocent graffiti brought the pavement to life.

I imagine that in times past, acerbic political commentary stole between the columns of serene clichés, then vanished without trace. Such trickling artistry could be indulged as a safety valve to release reproach as an ephemeral whisper.

And then, there is the secret calligraphy of marginalia and footnotes:

We had a banquet on Wednesday, at the 'World's Best Dumpling Restaurant' The noble house of Lao Bian Jiao Zi was established some 170 years ago, and now boasts over a hundred whimsical variations on the petite-pudding theme.

Generations of talented jiaozi-miesters, depicted in faded sepia daguerreotype, adorn the walls. Emperor Dao Guang was a fan; but alas, custom dictated that he could only gorge himself once a year, jiaozi being otherwise disparaged as poor man's food.

Hou Baolin, the late, great master of Chinese calligraphy, immortalised the humble dumplings in an inspirational scroll,

which declared *"Lao Bian jiaozi, No.1 in the world"*. And then, embellishing an otherwise unblemished reputation, the restaurant won the prestigious 'Golden Pod' award.

Certainly, the meal was very good indeed. Though by the final course, we had been so well and truly 'toasted', it could have been McDonalds. Drunk again; but only in the selfless pursuit of Sino-European détente. The sooner we let these guys into the WTO the better. Our hostess was the Business Manager for the Central District; a very spunky lady, who is now a firm friend, *"….whether we get the World Bank money or not"*.

A few days later, we were invited to dinner at her home. Madame Qin is clearly very senior in the Party and I imagine her support is not optional. All the same, one hopes her husband is not a violent man; the lady is a great cuddler.

We all had our fortunes told; the medium of portent being jiaozi soup. A waitress, who clearly majored in dumpling-lore, sampled the soup blind-sided. I scored seven – right off the one-to-six scale. And what do you know, just two days later, I became a rip-roaring success story. There you go; but then so did we all.

Mme Qin invited us to the official opening of the 'Shenyang Festival of Art and Calligraphy'. The 'round-eyes' sat at the top-table grinning stupidly behind large table-tags inscribed with the epithet: 'Our Esteemed Leaders'.

Our confusion was recorded in real-time by State Television. Ian rose to the occasion and gave a brief interview in halting Mandarin. Panama hat and shades; he could have been Philip Marlow. In the Star Hollywood bar, that evening, we became celebrities. Even Tony, the manager, abased himself.

The ephemeral art of Dishu is normally practiced with oversize calligraphy brushes. The Shenyang fountain pen variant is clearly a technological step up. 'Earth writing' using water is said to be a relatively new phenomenon first observed in this province. But, equally likely, it is just something that went unnoticed by the west – as with so much else in the Middle Kingdom.

The ephemeral art of Dishu is normally practiced with oversize calligraphy brushes. The Shenyang fountain pen variant is clearly a technological step up. 'Earth writing' using water is said to be a relatively new phenomenon first observed in this province. But, equally likely, it is just something that went unnoticed by the west – as with so much else in the Middle Kingdom.

Water calligraphy. Image - Chinapictures

Unbridled mains

2000, Argyll: Big country landscapes are magnificent, but the sheer scale of Alaska or among the big mountains of the Himalayas, for example, denies the essential element of progression – that constantly changing scenic dynamic that animates the landscape we pass through.

The Alps of Europe, by contrast, deliver 'progression' in spades. The landform is legible even among the highest peaks. So, while size matters, it is not always an asset; thus, landscapes are assessed by professionals in terms of 'relief amplitude' rather than scale.

The Highlands of Scotland are less dramatic than Austria, but our land is equally rich in incident and expression. In the Alps, the valley floor may be at 2,000ft; but our, more modest, mountains rise from sea-level to ragged snow-capped peaks and can evoke the same awe.

In this magical world of hills and glens you don't have to travel half-a-day to gain a new perspective on the countryside. There is tangible middle distance. You are close enough to 'the view' to see squalls ruffle the hillside and spume caper on the surface of the lochs.

As we travelled along Loch Lomond-side, a stiff north-easterly set up a continuous field of whitecaps to balance the gathered contours of a rising snowline. Narrow columns of rain, iridescent in the bright sunshine, enlivened a classic vista down the great length of the Loch.

To the east, the massive bulk of the Ben seared its powerful profile on the landscape – hot white against the cold blue sky. And on the near shore, the shattered summit of the Cobbler breached the horizon with a charge of raw authority.

I slowed right down to something approaching the legal limit and let it all soak in. It's always good to be back. Being at home, in this part of the world where outdoor sports are the staple leisure pursuit, made me realise that Samuel is living a cosseted urban life. But he will soon be old enough for adventures.

At 18 months, his sister Kathryn traipsed the ridgelines of Skye and Mull – an imperious jockey, riding aloft in a faded blue kiddy-carrier; chapped red cheeks and quilted red zoot-suite. She gibbered and gurgled and rubbed her runny nose into the back of my neck. Samuel has all this to look forward to.

As Mammon 'let's slip the dogs of war' and the tiger economies of Asia go global, the present merges with the future. But, in Scotland little had changed and, to be honest, most of that change has been for the better.

In Kilmun, we no longer have an American arsenal moored at the bottom of the garden, although there is still a sinister British nuclear bunker in a labyrinth of apocalypse-proof catacombs over the hill behind the house. Out of sight? On this side of the hill, yes. Out of mind? Mostly.

A bike-ride 'round-the-hill' on the forest tracks is an essential highlight of even a flying visit to the 'Anchorage'. This circular route starts behind the house and, for the first mile or so it traverses the hillside on a dirt-road pegged out by my father after the war, during his first professional job as an engineer with the Forestry Commission.

As kids, we used to toboggan and roll Easter eggs on these grassy lower slopes. Now, they are cloaked with a Sitka Spruce plantation – in dull middle age, like myself.

I rode past the site of the old stables. When I was a child, the forests were harvested without machines. Hard men worked in pairs, wielding terrifying axes and big crosscut saws. They took only prime timber and left only sawdust.

The logs pulled out by teams of heavy horses. My brother Norman and I would clamber up the hill at the end of the working day, to crouch behind the rough wooden shelter and peer through the cracks at these magnificent animals.

Splintered sepia rays from the low winter sun pierced the gloom, diffusing airborne hay-dust and guttural snorts of courser condensation. Through the splintered boards, we glimpsed unbridled mains, massive haunches, spade-sized hooves and latent strength. It's yet another image that stays with me.

Logging has changed. Few people work on the hills anymore and those who do sit in a heated cab listening to country and western music on the stereo, while a semi-autonomous multi-function arm fells, sneds, sections and stacks the lumber. These machines labour through the night under powerful arc-lights, becoming profitable only after midnight. They demand great skill in operation and leave behind a devastated hillside, almost impassable and open to erosion.

A parallel universe

2000, Liaoning: It is a parallel universe. Things are similar but not quite the same. The paradigm slippage of on-off isolation has not yet been re-centred by globalisation and international trade. So, for the moment, fascinating differences remain.

The denizens of the Orient are still different enough to challenge those long-established Western norms which are, perhaps, only conventions? Take Chinese lorries for example: trucks (even quite large ones) have just three wheels, motorcycle front-suspension, single-cylinder petrol engines and belt-drive transmissions.

The urban wasteland is different too; and it's well worth poking about. During a three-day public holiday spent on the roads of the city, I rode through the cantons of hope and despair. I pedalled out of town to the north-west and to the south-east. In both directions I found squalor on a level that transcends hopelessness. Much of rural China is still like this.

There is a simple equation: productivity must rise before incomes can follow. You can always produce more from the land with capital-intensive, yet relatively sustainable, techniques; but perhaps four out of five jobs in farming will disappear over the next couple of decades.

The corollary is rural depopulation on an unprecedented scale. And, coincidentally, it's also the PRC's long-standing strategy. The 9th Five-year Plan argued that: the flight from

rustic poverty to urban opportunity will fuel economic growth, drive up consumption, create new jobs and crank up the whole neo-capitalist process. This sounds suspiciously like perpetual motion to me – but then again, voodoo economics always does.

A better life through urbanisation? I see a different reality: Flat-pack mega-cities will coat the land like an oil slick. Scrappy little country towns will 'grow like Topsy' but the homes they provide will not be like Uncle Tom's Cabin.

Consider also the increasing polarisation of this society, as it undergoes the painful transition of industrial restructuring. Take these trends, strap a rocket to them, then 'light the blue touch-paper and retire'.

The result: subsistence urban economies rolled out by the linear kilometre, without regard to environment or quality-of-life. The game peasants have been sacrificed, hung and lightly fried. They now await the searing griddle. Fortunately, as consultants furthering the geo-political agenda of the European Commission, we were not being paid by results.

Of course, it's not all, all that bad. Consider life as a bike-ride. It is almost possible to loop Shenyang, between the first and second ring roads, along the banks of the main drainage canals. This route is made up of dedicated cycleways, paved footpaths, good dirt tracks and main-road detours in equal parts.

On the last day of Liaoning's ten-day spring, some of the most dilapidated stretches of urban dereliction were the most uplifting. Willow and cherry blossom rioted colourfully, and with exceptional abandon. New growth had yet to assume the dreary habit of summer grey.

Through the next six months, these plucky bushes and hardy trees will be ravished daily by dust clouds and coated with sticky airborne grime. The water-table will drop out of reach

through rock-hard laterite soils. Brittle roots will be forced to follow the merest trace of condensation, to test the integrity of the city's leaky reticulated infrastructure.

Plant-life is a hard life indeed in Shenyang.

The canals are a major asset, in an otherwise-grim industrial town, anchoring the city's greening programme. When open space, structural landscaping and recreational uses are physically linked, they become dramatically more effective.

With a little more investment (well, quite a lot more, to be honest), it could all come together. For the moment though, it's a bit worrying that, as new links are being constructed, earlier sections are falling into disrepair. While this does give challenging off-road cycling conditions in the city; that may not be the point.

Street theatre: Itinerant barbers are common enough everywhere in Asia, but street dentists? That one for sure is more entertaining. In the latter case, you'll find two stout ladies plying the trade: a 'wrestive' pair of pliers indeed.

They stand beside a rickety tricycle. The flat-bed is draped in white and daubed with blood-red signage. On the top, laid out splendidly on scarlet cloth there are just three tools: long-handle tongs, a skewer and what looks like a shifting-spanner.

One masked grandmother in a white coat is the dentist. The other, also in a white coat and usually more robust, is the anaesthetist; she holds you down. As I took a photograph, a third player, the patient, put on a brave face and smiled. Plucky fortitude redefines that expression. Brace yourself kids, now pull a face.

Missed photo-ops: Hard-by the smiling dental casualty, a peanut stand exploded with an impressive bang like mortar fire. It would have been a great picture, but I missed it waiting for the air to clear. There were peanuts everywhere. For a while, a thick cloud of smoke obscured the outcome. That, of course, would have been 'the photograph'.

The aftermath revealed nothing more than a blackened drum, with the bottom blown clean out of it, and a dazed and very sooty vendor. Later that day, I came across another small-disaster-cum-photo-opportunity at Beiling Park. An unattended three-wheeled taxi took off like a lifeboat towards the boating lake. I was ready for the big splash this time, with my camera poised, but the little motorised trike hit a tree on the way down.

I last visited China at Christmastime in 2014. In Beijing, the far horizon extended to a single city block. The streets were carpeted with late-model vehicles, nose-to-tail. On more than one occasion I abandoned my taxi to walk. Young millionaires with blank expressions and facemasks sat alongside in Ferraris and Lamborghinis. At intervals, they would back-up a line of traffic to leave 100m of clear road ahead to show off and burn rubber for a few seconds.

This used to be cycling heaven.

Shenyang, China. Image - the Author

Antediluvian transformers

2000, Liaoning: It rained last week. It doesn't rain here often. Hard rain from the rooftop scupper-drains spews a scummy cataract, to sweep the sidewalk and wash the streets. Outside my office window, self-important concrete pylons, skewed-wiff by industrial-strength frost-heave, two-finger the sky. Hawser-like power-lines dangle, downcast.

Alarming gangs of antediluvian transformers intimidate the street. Last week, one of these blew up, three times. And three times the Qing Dynasty fire engine from the Imperial Palace fire station, knee-knaad down through the drizzle to ponder the smouldering wreckage.

It was better than the fireworks on the City's 2300th birthday, a couple of weeks ago (yes, 2,300 years; this is China). There was a big bang, and nobody jumped. If only it were like that back home in Indonesia.

The next morning, we visited the Immigration Department to extend my visa. I am working here on a Tourist Visa, so this was not a 'formality' I was looking forward to. But no bribes were necessary; there were no problems at all in fact.

As befits a bureau on the international stage, there is a large wall map behind the service counter. The countries of the world are depicted in polished brass on blue hessian. There are a few small errors, however.

Ireland is the right way up, but the Scotland enjoys the warmth of more southerly geography and faces France across the Channel. Meanwhile, Cornwall braves the biting air of the

Minch and the bare midriffs of Essex shiver in the Hebrides. In the tropics, Java, Bali and poor wee Lombok have disappeared from the face of the earth.

The stealth archipelago is fading, island by island, drowning not waving as it goes under for the third time. I knew it would happen eventually. But then, when the immigration officials checked my hotel, it seems I had disappeared too; I wasn't registered there. So, at least we are all in the same extraterrestrial dimension.

Continuing on the themes of other worlds and other worldliness; it rained again yesterday. On most of my projects, there are drainage and flood control engineers. When it rains, they dive out the door delighted, and come back muddy and bedraggled, gushing with incredible-puddle stories.

Shenyang is primed for inundation. The roadside drains are 100 metres apart, and there is no fall on flat paved areas. The underground malls (it's extremely cold in the winter) and underpasses lack interceptor drains, so they flood too. And, of course, all the roofs leak. Water simply pours from light fittings in suspended ceilings.

The people are not prepared either. My fluorescent yellow 'Kag-in-a-bag' generated serial hilarity, as I rode past stranded crowds, without Macs or brollies. They clustered in doorways, like sweat bees on dank oxters. All this was a novelty, so I hope they were happy. I've had to wait years for a proper West of Scotland downpour, but it was worth it to be prepared.

Hard by the Trader's Hotel, there is a street of retail booths. As I cycled past this afternoon, a close-ranked parade of mannequins stood before them, exposed to the elements, sheltering under umbrellas and dressed in plastic bags. No one thought to haul these poor dummies inside.

Popcorn seller, Shenyang, China. Image - the Author

Sharkskin-suited Mafioso

2000, Liaoning: Shenyang had endured a long, hard and bitterly cold winter dipping beneath minus 20⁰C. This last week, the daytime temperature has crept slowly upwards through zero to reach plus 20⁰C, but some folks are still not convinced that summer has finally arrived.

There are only two seasons in Liaoning Province. The crossover is brief, but erratic. Thus, half the male population roam the streets well wrapped-up with two pairs of trousers, while the rest are already in the salary-man summer uniform of polyester slacks, white short-sleeved shirts and sunglasses.

The girls are a law unto themselves and are not so easy to stereotype. Some change into sensible sneakers for the morning commute, others pedal more precariously with platform-soles or spike heels.

Out on the bike-lanes, black sit-up-and-beg bicycles, like my mother used to ride, are the dominant genus. They are always ridden by young men-in-a-hurry, dressed alike with white socks and black slip-ons – colourful kipper ties fluttering in the wind of passage. They rip through the slow-moving peloton like barracuda among koi.

Cafes and restaurants have spilled out onto the sidewalk. In the evenings, splendidly incongruous Cinzano-type parasols now appear on the soiled pavement. It's almost festive. And, let's face it, eating out over a drain suits the Chinese style of dining, with its prodigious generation of debris.

It was a joy to revisit Beiling Park. There are countless kilometres of trails criss-crossing the park's 330 hectares – single-speed Nirvana. I went out fairly late in the afternoon. The lowering sun flooded the park with a golden glow, prolixed by a light particulate pollution.

The few cyclists you meet off-road ride sedately, bar the adolescent kids who tear through the backwoods like yobbos, with their loud singlets, baggy trousers, flapping denim shirttails, expensive sneakers and wrap-around sunglasses. Just like myself.

Off to school, Xingcheng, China. Image - the Author

Lifecycles

2000, Liaoning: A Chinese family enter the New World Hotel gym. They tune the four televisions to four separate channels. Mum nervously treads a 'Lifestride', hanging on grimly. Junior reclines on a 'Lifecycle', idly spinning one pedal with the resistance switched off. Dad just stands there transfixed beneath the TV, craning his neck to follow the US Open. After six minutes they retire en-masse to the steam room, exhausted. Is this a metaphor? And if it is, for what?

Meanwhile in Indonesia, Central Government has lost control over voracious regional governments, a rabid military and a demented population. Law and order have broken down, and the Judiciary functions only as a cynical Dutch auction. The nation's asset base and environment are being systematically looted. And the suppressed evil in society has risen to condense in a festering scab of sectarian militiamen.

If such chaos is really democracy, we may have to review the definition. Against this, the authoritarian government in China doesn't seem so bad. Unless, of course, they are bulldozing the bejesus out of unsightly slums; to tidy up a blot on the landscape; to effectively scupper the last refuge of the 'floating population'.

OK, I suppose I'm a slum-junkie. I love to cycle through the slums and absorb the humanity that transcends circumstance. But not just any old slums. They must be turn-of-the-century, pre-industrial or otherwise bijou slums, low-rise

inner-city neighbourhoods with quaint tiled roofs and a tasteful coherence. Slums where the condemned physical fabric cannot contain enduring social substance. Where both are lashed together with equal measures of grit and desperation

I must concede that my enthusiasm for urban areas blighted by distress and despair is horribly elitist and slightly obscene. There is no debate that the ragged quarters of Shenyang are unfit for human habitation. And, in mitigation, at work I adopt a pro-development frame of reference, beyond the pale from present day political correctness. I couldn't do my job, if not for that rationalist view.

Still, I am fascinated by the sight, the touch, the smell of everyday materials in terminal decay. In the sharply defined light-and-shadow of the afternoon sun, the slums of Shenyang transcended the difficult aesthetic of 'found materials'.

Even as these deprived communities push-shit-uphill, they humble our disquiet, with ingenuity and resourcefulness. Salvage is piled high along the margins of the road-to-ruin. The discarded detritus of more affluent districts is arrayed and, paradoxically, picked clean.

We can observe the building blocks of centuries – brick, timber and steel, decay, decompose and disappear gracefully. Warm tones of brown meld with cool tones of grey, as crumbling structures slump to ground at obtuse angles-of-repose, or rather I'm afraid repossession.

'On your bike' as they say at home: So, I cycled 'home', revelling in the buzz of the experience, and feeling slightly ashamed by the visceral intensity of my voyeurism.

Street scene, Shenyang, China. Image - the Author

Bewitching gravity

2000, Liaoning: Imagine this backstreet frontage, hidden and perhaps forgotten, somewhere behind our earnest four-star hotel. Rattling by on the bike, stirring the dust of ages, my peripheral vision brushes the random elements of a rich and varied streetscape: a restaurant, an ironmonger, a wide-mouthed furnace, a tailor, a hairdresser.

What?

Let's run that by again, an open-mouthed furnace? ....a Goddamned gaping furnace, licking the sidewalk with a roaring orange flame. There are several around here. As the proud owner of a Phoenix bicycle, I take a special interest in ashes. When I work it out I'll let you know.

Anachronisms aside, in China today folks have a lot more disposable income; the new-middle-class can go out and about in the evening and have a good time. But they still go home to a magpie's nest – one of a million tiny oases lodged deep in the bowels of the city.

Each little apartment is a 'good-life' simulator, insulated from the squalor of the real world by a virtual reality. A cheap concrete box is 'parqueted' and papered and stuffed with toys. The double-glazing is rose-tinted; the blinds are drawn. The television is the window, with a view that bridges the urban wasteland – to gain the remote prospect of a better life.

Here, the allure of the world-wide-web and transcendental telecommunications is inevitable. The day-to-day diet of the

city is already fortified with optic-fibre, and the population is even now metabolising it with barely a hiccup.

And not just 'here' of course: Each year, billions of hours of precious human life are surrendered to the bewitching gravity of the cathode ray tube. We have lost a generation, trapped forever in the fine print of the Web's gooey filament.

The Internet is a sleeping monster. Even as the Kraken still slumbers, it swells exponentially, draining the Blue Planet's vital life-force, with a truly mind-numbing transfusion of discarded intellect. Thus in 2044, all reality will be 'virtual', just as the last majestic Red Meranti hits the devastated deck of the world's last rainforest.

And they have abandoned their bicycles, which now pile up in great rusting heaps in the gloomy squalor of the backcourts behind the apartment buildings. Road-widening programmes have gobbled up the once-ubiquitous bike-lanes. The remaining cyclists now hazard pedestrians on the crowded sidewalks.

What a God-awful future.

Shenyang, China. Image - SUPP Team

The cabbage season

2000, Liaoning: And it's the cabbage season again. The poink, poink, poink, poink, poink, poink of single cylinder, tricycle trucks echoes in the sixteen-storey toilet-tiled canyon that leads to the back entrance of my hotel. Ancient, grime encrusted, agricultural vehicles slip into town after dark, laden with great mounds of long-eared vegetables.

Two 'horsepower' donkey carts bring up the rear; but they don't arrive until the early morning, after an eternal clip-clop, depressed beneath the almost-worthless product of distant acreage.

Back in the village, raggle-taggle tots eagerly anticipate the wretched returns from dad's annual excursion to the bright lights. It's the highlight of the year, whether you are the sorry ass impaled by the shafts or trotting in sublime resignation between them.

In the old days, the worthy cabbage kept scurvy at bay through the winter. Now, it's more of a tradition than a necessity. Pretty much everything is available now, year-round, in the supermarkets. Still, for the next few weeks, the city's alleyways will be carpeted and its balconies bestrung with the ubiquitous greens, before they are reduced to a sour pickle, like the rest of us.

And so, we run the gamut from cabbages to 'kringe'.

Argyll Forest Park. Image - Dawn McRae

Carraig-na-Maraig

2000, Argyll: After a summer break in Britain, I always need a little time to come to terms with the stultifying constraints of a largely desk-bound profession. The paradox of any career progression is that, while we may have started out doing things we enjoy, we all end up doing much the same thing – attending pointless meetings and making arbitrary decisions.

I find myself increasingly reluctant to capitulate to the office routine; especially, since I was able to get out on the bike for two or three hours nearly every day during the month when we were home in Scotland. Most of these rides were comfortable reruns of favoured circuits, but some individual incidents bear recalling.

Scott, an old cycling buddy from Indonesia, came down from Aberdeen. Keen to show him Cowal biking at its best, I introduced him to the Glendaruel – Glenmassan 'loop'. This is not so much of a loop as a bush-whacking opportunity.

We completed much of the 'wilderness gap' by way of the upper reaches of the River Massan, after I lost the intermittent sheep-track we were following. There had been heavy rain and so the stream's brisk torrent helped us on our way. In fact, our slither down the bed of the icy cataract was a welcome break after an interminable squelch over miles of moorland, through deep, black, sticky ooze.

A few days later, I had a crack at an apparently feasible variation of a loop bordering the 'Rest-and-be-thankful' climb in the company of Chris, a partner in crime since childhood. The waymarked route is a hard ride which encompasses seven big hills and boasts stunning views. However, it is currently closed because the 'saddle trail', a key single-track section of the route recently built by the National Parks Authority, is impassable. I suppose that should have told us something.

First attempt, anti-clockwise: In light but enervating drizzle, we pedal along well-maintained forest tracks, down the east shore of Loch Goil and past the fork to the now off-limits saddle trail, to arrive at Carraig-na-Maraig – the road-end. It is immediately obvious why the road 'breaks' at this point on the Ordinance Survey map. The headland before us is more-or-less vertical.

Still, all is not lost. From the end of the trail, two alternative routes appear to present themselves. One, with a ropy-looking handrail, leads on and down, around a vestigial ledge on the cliff face, the other zigzags straight up on our left flank. This treeless hillside is fairly 'exposed', with nothing to impede a rapid, rather-bouncy and no-doubt-fatal descent to the dull-grey waters of Loch Goil, a couple of hundred feet below.

We go up. The grassy slope is steep but usefully tussocky. As long as we don't slip, and as long as the rumpled blanket of topsoil doesn't begin to slither off the hillside altogether, we will be ok. No problems then; we trudge up shouldering our bikes, although when I get to the top and look back down, I feel slightly sick. Exposure, especially on surfaces with the friction coefficient of wet grass, does that to me.

Chris, on the other hand, used to do this stuff for a living – before he succumbed to the beguiling indulgence of full-time yachting. And indeed, his climbing skills will be an especially useful asset on a second, later attempt and will, to some extent, redeem his spin on our navigational roulette this time out.

Suddenly, as often in this part of the world, the mist closes in. Complacency, My Lord, is our only defence. In the gloom, we lose sight of Carrick Castle, which was our main point of reference. And then we lose every other reference, foresights and back-sights both. Imposing bluffs and alarming precipices now seem to define our horizon on all sides. In such entrancing conditions, callow ramblers and gung-ho lemmings get lost every season in the Scottish Highlands, although generally at much higher altitudes.

So, I place myself in the capable hands of a certified mountain leader. However, I do this with some reservations, as I privately find his chosen heading more than a little suspect. An hour or so later, we catch sight of a road. It looks like the one we just left, but no matter. As a working hypothesis, we agree to assume otherwise and head in that direction. This is just fine until the steep heather gives way to vertical rock at the road cutting. So near and yet…. etc.

Buoyed up by the two-fold delusions of groundless anticipation and self-deception, we scramble along the crumbling edge looking for a way down. This is a hard struggle, dragging the bikes through increasingly dense and thorny vegetation.

It occurs to me that cycling shorts are not a good idea on Scottish hillsides as my legs are now liberally lacerated. Chris, the bastard, is wearing long hiking pants over the top. At last, we chance upon an exit chute. By this time, we have traversed far enough to unequivocally recognise our original point of departure.

Second attempt, five days later, clockwise, which Chris suggests will be more committing and thus, somehow, to be preferred. It is an overcast and blustery morning. We set out on the circuit once again, this time with a map. We 'band of brothers', though in the twilight of our athletic prowess, have some unfinished business to attend to here.

Jaws set, we engage the foothills of Ben Dornish and grind the length of Gleann Mar. A long and steady gradient delivers us to a high-point above the 'Rest-and-be-thankful' pass. At the top, we turn right and cruise down Glen Croe beneath the repine north-east face of the Brack. Then, we hang right again to follow Loch Long on a new path recently constructed between high-level logging roads by the ever-helpful Forest Enterprise.

Encouraged by this unanticipated short-cut, Chris and I press on south. After that first abortive reccé, we reckon we are well-set-up to take on the Carraig-na-Maraig gap. Well, yes and no. The road ends and the landscape is immediately familiar. We had come within 50 yards of this place on the previous attempt. In fact, everything is now clearly laid out before us, since we are standing on the edge of yet another sheer rock-face and looking straight down on a small plateau.

Chris confidently shoulders his bike and strides over the edge. I hope he has seen something I haven't, because I know for sure he didn't pack a parachute. But fortune favours the brave. In an unlikely scenario, a new (black, flecked with silver) fixed rope has been bolted down the wall, most likely by one of the many outdoor education centres that take advantage of this rather special landscape.

For us, it makes the difference between, 'Plan A', a brisk 42 klicks followed by a pub lunch, and 'Plan B', doubling back for a stomach-rumbling 75km off-road slog. I lower my bike on our emergency tether, and then nervously skitter down the fixed rope. The hard-plastic soles of SPD shoes, shod with protruding steel cleats, are not ideal for rock climbing.

Even from here, we lose the track and end up, once again, in tangled bush above the road cutting. But this time, that's good enough.

Tetrapack milk-cartons

2000, Bali: We are trundling down the runway of the N'gura Rai Domestic Airport. A fellow passenger glances over his shoulder, back through the unsecured rear door to the cargo hold. This guy is completely thrown by a momentary view of Jimbaran Bay.

The boxy little Shorts SC.7 Skyvan aeroplane used on the milk-run across the Lombok Strait was built in Belfast. It appears to have been modelled after a Tetrapack milk-carton, so the whole back end unfolds. Someone has forgotten to refold the tail and my bike is among a chaotic heap of bags shortly to be strewn across Nusa Dua.

An impromptu bombing sortie over the magical mountains of Bali would have been worth it, just for the story. But sadly, alarmed by the prospect of losing his toothbrush, the less-than-sanguine tourist sitting behind me makes a quick dash up the isle to the cockpit to petition the flight crew.

A switch is thrown, and a hidden panel appears from nowhere to clang shut just before 'V2 – rotate – dump the luggage'. Who would have conceived an inward opening hatch, top hung from the rear edge, which sweeps through half the enclosed space?

Meanwhile, in Jakarta, the rakyat bopped in unison to the beat of another 6.5 Richter. This nearly always happens when I am away from home. Samuel's alphabet play-mat was inundated by a freak tidal wave which doused his favourite toys before trucking on down the hall to refill the half-empty fishpond. It's weird; we only notice earthquakes when the pool empties itself.

Head well protected, Lombok. Image - the Author

Lombok skies. Image - the Author

The South-west Monsoon

2001, Lombok: Wham! The muggy warmth has gone, quite suddenly. The South-west Monsoon is doing the other thing it does well. It's blowing like buggery, carrying away tables and chairs and remoulding the foreshore. The beach is now billowing and unblemished, sculpted in soft contours. It's the first time I've seen spindrift in Lombok – on the swimming pools. That's a serious draught.

I stayed in last night, as the hotel is one of the few spots in town with a reliable generator. I dined apprehensively in the beachside pizza restaurant, visualising the destructive violence of shredding plate-glass, even though I was well away from the creaking windows on the exposed weather elevation. There were at least three power-cuts during dinner, so it was a good decision.

And so far, it has been a lazy Sunday, stretched out, watching the breeze bedraggle the coconut trees by my balcony. Indeed, the roar of solid air, driven through thrashing palm fronds, is about the only noise that can compete with the crash of the surf. Meanwhile, my little travelling hi-fi is wheezing breathlessly, out of its league in such boisterous company.

What to do in this weather?

Head for the heights, raise two fingers to the glowering sky and defy the elements. I pedalled out to a promising valley, where we have dithered around the lower reaches on the Friday evening mixed-Hash runs. My initial plan was to follow a

tributary of the Kali Meninting to its source, then loop round to the left and exit along a remembered broad-backed bluff.

But somehow, before reaching the headwaters, the trail panned out to the right, then zigzagged more-or-less straight up into a wood, identified by the remains of a rotting wooden signboard as a 'Protected Forest'.

I blunder breathlessly up the slope, driven before the nimble wit of a local comedian. In Lombok, these wizened old wags may simply materialise, like shamans – which maybe they are. This jungle-jester egged me on with gleeful derision, as he capered impetuously in my wake, beneath a weighty beam of coconuts.

I could have wrapped that yoke around his neck.

Eventually, we gained our objective, and I could mount-up and drop the old boy at last. It was an outstanding knife-edge ridge with spectacular views over the entire southern half the island.

The summit path was spectacular, if disconcertingly narrow and exposed. Still, it was ridable and the alang-alang grass helpfully obscured the precipitous drop-offs. But then, almost cruelly, this bulwark flattened across the track with each nuclear gust, to trigger a glorious wave of heightened sensory perception.

Up there on that isolated ridge, protected by five kilometres of hard climbing at one end and a giddy flight of rudimentary steps on the other, there were a few precious klicks of some of the most wonderful mountain biking I have experienced anywhere. When the force is with you….

These are the kind of spiritual trails that prompt you to abuse the bike and scream euphoric invectives into the teeth of an oblivious gale. It was a major vertiginous high. There is something wonderful about taking wheeled vehicles into

regions where they are not just a novelty for the locals, but completely unknown.

The day closed out prematurely, however, when I chewed up the derailleur hanger traversing a mattress of windblown debris. And then, when I rebuilt the transmission as a single speed, it obstinately returned to the 19th of 24 possible combinations and condemned me to pedal home, legs a blur, like a maniacal circus dwarf.

The typhoon is a genuine novelty too in this 'land below the wind'. There is a decaying tropical storm south of here, drawing its last breath while it cruises across Australia's 'top end'. As it unwinds, it bleeds into another, smaller typhoon, still vigorous and parked in the gap between there and here. Together, they are turbo-charging the regular airstream, through a complex series of geared interactions, to create the most powerful northerly breeze anyone can remember.

In effect, these depressions have evacuated about ten thousand square miles of the inter-tropical convergence zone, and the sky above Nusa Tenggara is pouring into that hole. I guess, this explains the lack of atmosphere in most of the bars along the strip this month.

The provincial capital of Mataram, on the other hand, has come alive with the rasp of chain saws, and now begins to resemble a logging camp. Government offices have been shorn of their pompous array of redundant signage and, in a divine masterstroke, every last one of the big lollipops advertising the new McDonalds has been humbled, blown flat at the neck to form giant bird-tables.

World Weather on CNN missed the implications of the two weather systems entirely, but the master-mariner who 'runs', or in this instance 'suspends' marine operations for the Newmont Mining Company in Sumbawa, gave the bar-props the full isobaric account. Over the weekend, I had been mesmerised by huge breaking waves, sliding down the Strait. It transpires that everyone else in the bar at Café Cherry had been gazing at the awesome bumps on the horizon too. Our guru confirmed that these are indeed respectable, Southern-Ocean-type swells, with enough authority to salt Grant Dalton's coffee.

Before the margins of this onslaught, the beach at the south end of the bay has completely disappeared. It has been undercut to the treeline to leave a five-metre face. Along much of the rest of the coastline, a surfeit of stockpiled jukong outriggers now perch precariously above a long drop.

And that, for once, has everything to do with 'the price of fish'.

Fishing bike, Lombok, Indonesia. Image - the Author

Lower regions of mild discomfort

2001, Argyll: I didn't do much when I was home on leave. But I did feel obliged to honour a promise to myself and go for a decent bike-ride. So, on the back of a few days of cross-training – trimming holly hedges and hacking back rambling bush – I had a second crack at my now-to-be-annual century.

I slipped out the house at first light with a small Camelback, a bottle of orange squash and four Mars Bars – a rejuvenating confection now sadly a shadow of its former substantial self. It was a glorious morning with almost no wind. The sky was palest blue and innocent of cloud. It was perfect.

From Kilmun, I pedalled north, past Loch Eck and through the lower regions of mild discomfort, slowly unravelling muscles still knotted after a week's gardening. At St. Catherines, the rising contours soaked up my last few inches of gearing and I turned back. I made a mental note to replace my rear cluster with an 'alpine block', like wimpy associates Jim and Alan.

The roads were still empty as I doubled the shoreline section of Loch Fyne, to touch Strachur for the third time, before cruising back south. On then, down to Dunoon and past the knoll of Highlan' Mary – a milestone gobbled symbolically as Mars Bar No.1.

From there, I followed the shore-road to Toward, exited the Highlands briefly at the southern tip of the Cowal Peninsula, and rolled on up Loch Striven to the road-end – doubling-back with another three-point turn of corporeal, spiritual and cerebral inflection – an excuse for Mars Bar No.2.

And so back to Kilmun, now battling a risible headwind down the Dalilongart Straight while mainlining Mars Bar No.3. I passed our house with the odometer blinking through 90 miles; only five miles to Ardentinny and five more back, to conclude a pleasant morning and a relatively easy shoreline-century.

But then, at Blairmore Pier, hard on the sticky tail of Mars Bar No.4, I got a flat. Five minutes to change the tube, but ten more to blow it up to 110psi with my pocket-pump. By Loch Long, it struck me, as it often does, that I hadn't checked the inside of the tyre for the snag. Anyway, this time it held, and I made lunch at the Kilmun Hotel with the day's delegation of second, third and fourth cousins.

Useless facts: I understand that, not only do they come in a myriad of different sizes, but there are 42 different recipes for Mars Bars throughout the world, with the Belgian confection rated the finest. I take this as another affirmation of the numerical quotient of life.

Cycling Round the Hill, Cowal, Scotland. Image - GoPro still, the Author

Playing possum

2001, West Java and Shenyang: Samuel had been looking forward to Halloween for at least two weeks. Not that he needs a special occasion to masquerade behind wide-eyed innocence and play pranks on the household. Teddy-bear-faced cheek at the scene of the crime is his stock in trade.

Halloween is also his birthday. Each year, the toothy glow of a million turnip lanterns warps us over the event-horizon. He is now three years old and understands that birthdays bring presents, cakes, ice cream and the opportunity to push his luck.

So, he was looking forward to it. Every morning on the run-in to his anniversary he asked to be hoisted aloft to see his presents. They were bundled in a big red plastic carrier bag and wedged inaccessibly atop the wardrobe in the spare bedroom. The new bike, of course, was hidden elsewhere.

Then, the night before the Big Day the boy was as sick as a puppy. Even so, next morning, he got dressed up to go to school in his sorcerer's apprentice waistcoat, which custom dictates that he can only wear once a year on his birthday.

But I'm afraid it was never really on. When I came downstairs for breakfast he was already wilting. Bar a brief trip to the local health centre, he spent the entire day spread-eagled, playing possum out on the patio. It all stemmed from an episode playing principal goat in his favourite panto: 'The Three Billy Goats Gruff'. He successfully duped the wicked old troll and gained the greener pastures on the other side of the bridge.

Alas, goats eat grass.

Poor wee Samuel. He had a miserable birthday – contemplating the meaning of life and wallowing in alarming hypotheses. When Alison came home, he told her in a small voice: "*Mum, Mum, my birthday isn't working Mummy. I think I'm dead Mum. I'm soooo dead.*"

And a little later, I overheard: "*Are you dead too Mummy, or just very, very old?*"

In fact, it wasn't his week. On Samuel's first day back at school, two thugs on a 125cc Suzuki motorcycle cancelled the tiny-tots swimming lessons with a fragmentation grenade. For this cowardly act of sickening malevolence, we can credit the Coalition's elevation of Osama bin Laden to the status of prophet.

This bin-man is not content piling-up the refuse of discontent, he now aspires to head the blacklist of bogeymen in every secular state. He condemned Australia's support for East Timor's cessation from Indonesia as a 'crusade'. So, a jihad has been cobbled together in response and these sons-of-bitches bombed the Australian International School.

As a proviso to the shabby agenda of the 'New Apocalypse', that makes sense. Guilt, it seems, is lightly borne and never ridden. An almighty explosion blasted a big hole in a concrete wall and broke a few windows.

I'm reluctant to credit the grace of God in this most providential of possible outcomes. Christ, it's a kiddies' school. Still, today the Australian International School is probably the safest place in town. The campus cowers behind sky-scraping mesh and a cordon of thirty-odd police clad in flak-jackets and armed with M16s.

We've kept the toy-box free of dinky weaponry, although I suppose it won't be long before Samuel finds out about real

119

guns now. But Jesus, let him at least remain ignorant for aa few years about what they are for.

By contrast, now back in Shenyang, life goes on as normal. We are as far removed from this month's hastily arranged celebrity death match between the world's two great religions as might be contrived, geo-politically speaking. Even so, we had a visit from the local police last week, to advise us on basic security and how to spot anthrax in the mail. I suppose it's the same everywhere.

Will we ever get out of this mess? Will dogged pedantry triumph over recidivist fanaticism? Will reason prevail? Don't hold your breath; don't even stay tuned.

Meanwhile, small advances in evolution shore up both the human condition and our sustainable future. Samuel has ascended to the grownups' toilet. He burst onto the phone last Sunday to tell me that he had already christened three bathrooms and was eagerly anticipating a visit to the remaining two. He was thrilled to bits and so was I.

A quarter gill of euphoria rattled my skull and tickled my ears. It says a lot about the current state of the planet when a little boy's toilet training lights up the day. It was the best news I'd heard in a long, long time.

On two wheels, Jakarta, Indonesia. Image - the Author

Endless summer

2001, Lombok with memories of Nepal: Endless summer has returned to this island paradise. The naked sun now sears unprotected flesh through the wide-angle lens of a clear blue sky. Humidity has plummeted and the desiccated air around me is pushing remorselessly past 40 degrees. The island's smaller rivers have gathered up their lower reaches and retreated bodily into the shady foothills.

I aspire to that wisdom. On Sunday morning, I fell sound asleep under the rustling palm fronds of a coconut tree and awoke with a dappled patchwork of painful tattoos lasered across my chest. The malevolence of shadows; who would have thought?

With my bike buggered after mangling the derailleur last weekend, I've been condemned to roam the Senggigi highlands as a mere pedestrian. Here, on the Equator, Sol draws a blackout over his vassal world at 6.15 p.m. promptly each evening, eliminating dusk's margin for error.

Now, if you are benighted in the mountains on a bicycle, with ten minutes of gloaming and an even chance, you can bail out of almost any situation successfully to escape the summary sanction of the setting sun. On foot, you are toast.

I was up on the hills behind the hotel, contouring the sheer slopes at the head of the Batu Bolong gorge. I jogged along just below the summit ridge at 6.00 p.m. with something of a logistical challenge. I needed to lose about 200 metres before curfew, and quickly. Retracing my steps entailed a treacherous scramble and the best part of an hour.

So, the hunt was on for an emergency exit. I met a couple of people scurrying home for supper, but could I find anyone who spoke Indonesian? I realise now that I need to learn some rudimentary Sasak. Because, if you stray off the track, the chances are you will be in for an uncomfortable night in the open, or perhaps, a rapid and uncontrolled descent into oblivion.

Eventually, ferreting around in an apparently deserted hamlet, I startled a schoolboy in uniform and began the usual conversation of non-sequiturs. Senggigi Beach, it seemed, wasn't perhaps the best place to go, starting from here at this time in the evening. Aghhhh! Never mind, at last I had directions and I was earth-bound like a bouncing-bomb.

On Sunday, I tramped a more ambitious route to link the far ridges. And I realised how lucky I was to get down in one piece the last time. Walking the skyline is of course much easier than ploughing a transect against the grain of the landscape.

The 'Roosevelt Walk' is an exercise in pointless bloody-mindedness, bequeathed to an indifferent nation by an ex-president, who also gave his name to an entire genus of cuddly toys. When you walk the 'walk', you blunder blindly forward on a compass bearing and confront obstacles which sensible people can easily avoid. A straightforward scramble becomes a life-or-death adventure.

In this context, being scared of heights is an advantage in some ways. Paradoxically, that sinking feeling of unalloyed apprehension heightens the hill-walking experience. I usually return to sea level, strung-out and breathless – pathetically grateful just to be back down. The locals have addressed this syndrome by planting up the margins of the most intimidating paths to create a secure trench fenced in with living ramparts.

Isolated huts are set deep into the hillside below the ridgelines. These are the homes of a highly marginalised population – subsistence farmers, still living in the Iron Age. As with the paths, the necessary earthworks are buttressed and consolidated by extensive planting.

The island's mountain dwellers have developed some highly effective bio-engineering techniques. Stripped of their vegetation, these barely consolidated hills would slump to earth like a wet sandcastle. Fortunately, that's unlikely to happen. If you lean on your walking stick for more than a few minutes, it will take root and grow.

There are few domestic animals in the high villages, but there are plenty of chickens. Chickens are bold mountaineers. Many years ago, I traced the pilgrim's path to the polychromatic lakes of Panch Pokhari, with the Himalayan Hash House Harriers. From there, we tried to run competitively at altitude. Suffice to say it wasn't easy.

Only the hens, among a veritable Noah's Arc of livestock that began the trek with us, made it to the top. We ate the sacred cows between two and three thousand metres, then the mountain goats were all polished-off by the 4,000 metre-mark.

British Army squaddies carried our beer up as a training exercise. With 150 participants and 250 porters, the genesis 'Hash-trek' had a fair old appetite and a not inconsiderable thirst. Unfortunately, the army's munificence extended only so far – we were limited to just three beers each at the high camp.

It also struck me that chickens speak the same language the world over. These underestimated creatures no doubt laughed their heads off in cynical disbelief as they watched events unfold at Babel. However today, it's the laconic society of chickens who remain misunderstood, and are I suppose, if truth be told, still less than adept at keeping their heads.

Anemones in bondage

2002, Liaoning: Outside my window, a mock battle of terrifying intensity is being waged. The blitzkrieg is unrelenting. The ground shakes and my fragile fortress trembles. Fire engines race to douse scorched earth as blazing star-shells fall to ground. Continuous detonations lay down a carpet of rolling thunder and suck the atmosphere dry.

Powerful searchlights have been mounted on turrets and cornices around the perimeter of Zhongshan Square. They laser wild helical patterns across the night sky. For a brief instant, the beams expose the menacing grey bellies of Martial Hades' low-level bombers. On pyrotechnic nights such as this, the phantom squadron is released from interlunar purgatory to taunt the ghost of Marshall Zhang.

Shenyang regards the spectre with the jaundiced eye of a captive audience in the theatre of war. Still, they know the score. Across the city a barrage of ack-ack responds. The gunfire thunders to a climax, blending into a continuous blitzkrieg. The noise is deafening. It's hard to order a drink, neigh impossible. Tonight, the masses are unbridled. Inevitably, it's the Year of the Hoarse.

We have been making friends in the city. Zhang Dan is an avant-garde sculptor. This comes as something of a shock. Her muse is veiled. To be more precise, though we now threaten to bankrupt the metaphor entirely, she wears a gauzy purdah of suspended disbelief, wrought with a quizzical smile.

Smile, you're on 'Candid Karma'.

Dan's smile, 'mei kai yan xiao' can be loosely translated as 'the eyebrows relax and the eyes smile'. The Chinese are particularly graphic in their description of smiles:

☺ 'xiao' – a straightforward, honest-to-goodness beamer

☺ 'gui-xiao' – a beguiling smile

☺ 'kuang xiao' – a ravishing smile

☺ 'chau-xiao' – a laughing smile

☺ 'da-xiao' – a crinkly grin

☺ 'wei-xiao' – a tight wee smile

☺ 'leng-xiao' – a sardonic smile

☺ 'ku-xiao' – a wry smile

☺ 'ning-xiao' – a leer

☺ 'sa-xiao' – a silly smirk

And my special favourite: 'pi xiao rou bu xiao' – 'the skin is smiling, but the meat isn't'.

David and I hosted a joint birthday party for the EU project team at Zhang Dan's stylish restaurant-cum-art-gallery. It was a great success. Fe-5-O-fum. Dan presented us with a fabulous cake. It was the size of an occasional table, layered with fruit and encrusted with roses. It was also blessed with enough firepower to scorch the ceiling.

At its nub, a big plastic flower, which opened to reveal a candle on each petal and a corolla shot through with a blowtorch. Then, the device struck up a metallic chorus of 'Happy Birthday'. It was great; I'm a sucker for novelties.

March is a good month here. The equinoctial breeze blows the pollution away. I can see clear through Shenyang, across the capricious skyline of mad-capped post-modern towers and beyond to the countryside. The air is clean, and the pale blue sky is translucent. Pot-bellied clouds hover aloft like dirigible piglets.

Unlikely, granted, but on such a clear spring morning, the City is photogenic. I imagine a battalion of communist party photographers has been dispatched to capture a battery of misleading images – to wit, to shoot the pixels at the bottom of the garden. I hope they are well wrapped-up; spring or not, it's damn cold out on the bike today.

Even after all this time, I'm still not sure what we are all doing here in China; possibly, no one does; possibly, no one cares. It's a grim city, but the hospitality is matchless. As is apparent from these letters, we are fêted like rock stars. So, the weeks merge and flow one to another – celestial dreamtime bridges long unaccounted-for periods, even while events overlap and repeat.

Hence the abiding bewilderment.

Motorised mountain-bike, China. Image - the Author

Urban badlands

2003, Liaoning: It's been warm recently; but today I woke up to a blizzard. I also woke up with a heavy cold – almost routine on the adrenaline crash that follows the submission of a cellulose mountain of technical reports. So yes, we have finished here. There is a follow-on project in the works which will run through December 2003, but I am not so interested in that.

This morning, we went along to Shenyang Television to view the first cut of 'The Film'. It's great. The editing is very Chinese; very choppy, very gung-ho. Shenyang is going places; this is a city where it's all happening. But, before we get carried away, the credits roll (or would if they were there yet) and it's back to reality – mildewed concrete and urban badlands.

Still, this was a real effort to showcase the secondary heritage buildings from the 1930s. There is more to the social history of China than the Ming Dynasty. In this way, we hope to deter the wreaking-crews, as they wait in the wings for the warmer weather.

I have had my head down, rattling the keyboard, with one eye on CNN, but we have been out and about at weekends. In my 51st year I clambered up onto the saddle and rode a real-live horse for the very first time. Initially, the experience is insecure, bumpy, and rather smelly; but after a while all that passes. Now I know that horses are more comfortable by far than elephants, but no real competition for a good bicycle. And the raison d'etre for the exercise: I can now talk to Samuel, Marlboro-man to Marlboro-man, about this plan of his to become a cowboy.

Blood-spattered Bedlam

2003, West Java: Almost every time I leave the family alone in Indonesia, Jakarta becomes a blood-spattered Bedlam. Is family-life here still tenable? I just don't know. Certainly, with five bombs in Jakarta this year, and in view of the nature of the last one, we have some hard thinking to do. "*If you can keep your head when all about you are losing theirs and blaming it on you.*" So, wrote Kipling in 'If' and it was never more apt.

The Marriott Hotel's suicide bomber was readily identified when they found his severed head on the 5th floor of the hotel. It's as near Heaven as he's going to get. And if perchance there isn't a Hell, I'd be happy to subscribe to its construction. There is no earthly punishment commensurate with such crimes.

Traffic flows freely, a small mercy in the circumstances. We have been avoiding foreign-owned property, foreign gatherings and foreign watering-holes for some years in any case. Even so, there is always the nagging question at the back of my mind: what have we not taken account of; what did we not consider?

Latent hazards are pretty much everywhere, but we can still enjoy the countryside en famille on our bikes – something which the good people in the mined territories of Vietnam, Cambodia and Laos cannot do. Samuel can keep up now; well mostly, but he does sometimes just sit down and refuse to budge. His favourite part of the sport is to get up on the roof-rack when we load-up the bikes.

It's the condiments that kill

2003, Liaoning: Shenyang's heavy industries make poor-quality products that no one wants. Workplaces are unsafe, and factories spew toxic pollution hazarding the health of the entire nation. Restructuring the old manufacturing base is a huge challenge. I find myself back here in the smog with a small input in an industrial area restructuring project; the smaller the better – some of our team members are completely out of their depth.

Meanwhile, the informal economy in Shenyang is booming. Every evening at 5.30 as I leave the office the sidewalks undergo a process of transformation, to become an enormous outdoor market. The stalls arrive as great stacks of tubular frames laced with steel mesh.

In just twenty minutes, they are assembled and groaning under mounds of ten-a-penny merchandise. Then the barrow-boy convoys arrive en masse, bicycle wagon-trains of fat-bodied cartoon Conestogas, with flouncy canopies and wacky-racer wheels.

Outdoor retail floor-space may have doubled since last year. It seems to be a new take on 'cannibal competition' as everyone sells the same stuff. But hey, it's cheerful. Shenyang is half-way through a programme to reallocate the city's paved surfaces. Chinese politicians want a 'modern' city. So the transport planners are removing the cycleways and driving cyclists off the road onto the chaotic sidewalks.

Even so, business is uninterrupted.

Convicts in orange overalls labour to dig up and relocate the tangle web of reticulated infrastructure that lies beneath the streets. There are many things you can spend international loan money on, but the local authority seems to be 'unaware' that this is not one of them. No matter, 'trusties' queue for take-aways and an egalitarian lunch is served among the rubble in the shade of recycled Cinzano brollies. Sang-froid is a defining characteristic of the people here.

Foreign experts, all too often the victims of syncretic pragmatism, are frequently surprised by the pace of change in China. More often than not, we find that proposals tabled for discussion are already under construction. Once decisions are made – in this case to more-or-less rebuild an entire city – things happen incredibly fast.

During the summer, Shenyang endured another orgy of demolitions, jerry-built redevelopment and road-widening schemes. The old place looks better, certainly. But with each makeover, its character and down-at heel charm is, by stages, erased. It's not easy to cross the road now either, with 10 lanes of imperious traffic sweeping past on unblemished new asphalt.

The bike-lanes are almost gone now, but I am glad to have ridden through the pre-dawn of the brave new world. As China races into the future, there is bound to be collateral damage. It's just a pity that one day, and probably in the not-too-distant future, they will want to bring the bike-lanes back.

Like the rest of my colleagues, I wander the streets at weekends, to take the newly laundered air. The old Shenyang Station, famed site of the 'incident' leading to Japan's annexation of Manchuria, is currently under renovation. They seem to be doing a pretty good job; perhaps the message is getting through.

The Mukden pretext made the Chinese 'rustbelt' famous before organised crime stole the show. More recently, a new

generation of sticky-fingered bannermen have hogged the headlines in the print media. Corrupt politicians can expect little leeway or leniency here. On these increasingly frequent occasions when the coffer dams cave in, capital punishment accompanies capital flight.

However, despite an exhausting clean-up, the lads from the local 3K Triad still appear to be conducting business as usual, maybe even better than usual. The old Caddys and Plymouth Town Cars have been replaced with late-model Mercs and Beemers. Down by the station a big 7-series, with testosterone sweating from beneath the wheel arches, blocked the sidewalk. Close by a big Honda SUV, chariot-of-choice for the 'Praetorian Guard', blocked its exit.

Behind the tinted windows of the Honda, Al Pacino was emphasising an uncompromising line of argument in the usual way. As fast as I could avert my eyes – breakneck speed in this instance – for a moment, my fleeting glance was drawn down the barrel of a loaded .38 automatic.

"*We may find in the long run that tinned food is a deadlier weapon than the machine-gun.*" so said George Orwell in 'The Road to Wigan Pier'. Maybe George, but it's the condiments that kill, as this bizarre story, also making it into the papers this month, attests.

A gruesome chemical arsenal has been unearthed just north of here in Heilingjiang Province. At the latest count, thirty-six honest but simple folk have been hospitalized as a result of exposure to World War II mustard gas. They may take a long time to die. This unlucky region has seen chemical warfare unleashed by both US and Japanese forces within living memory.

Workers at a construction site in Qiqihar stumbled across some old steel barrels, buried for nigh-on sixty years. Being understandably curious, the lads knocked one over. It burst

open and an oily compound seeped into the soil. Later that evening, two yet more enterprising souls returned to the spot, emptied the remaining barrels and cut them up. They sold the scrap metal to an informal recycling facility in a nearby residential area.

And if that wasn't bad enough, the very next day, contaminated soil from the very same building site was carted off and spread throughout eleven separate locations. The Japanese have been invited back to deal with this horror show. They brought thirty-six bouquets of flowers to PLO Hospital No.203, but I suspect somehow that that won't be enough.

By contrast, this next disaster was entirely home-made. The story was recounted to me by a convivial professor of agriculture at the bar of the Holiday Inn.

Many places in Liaoning use industrial sewerage for irrigation purposes. The authorities are trying to phase the practice out, since the juicier the produce, the closer it comes to lethal. Watermelons are off the menu, then. However, there are other downsides that no one thought of.

Imagine the scene out on the rice padi: It's a sweltering day in early August. A couple of local worthies are spinning a yarn around fading recollections of the 'Great Leap Forward'. From time-to-time, they offer gratuitous advice to the contingent of young lads squelching stoically through the tedium of an industrial retraining scheme. The boys are learning the agri-business from scratch.

One of the old revolutionaries reaches into his pocket for a battered cigarette packet. The other acknowledges the treat and courteously lights-up; then, he toys with the still-burning match, as smokers do. In fact, a long moment draws out, until time stands still. Then, he flicks the tiny incendiary – in slow motion – towards the flooded field.

Wooomph! A blue flash sucks the air from the sky and snuffs out the newly lit fags. All around, neophyte farmers are borne aloft on the blast. They fall to earth and flounder weakly in the mud like stunned mullets, hair frazzled, clothes smouldering and faces scorched. Not since the Vietnam War has a padi field exploded in such a fashion. And yes, it's a true story.

With the warmer weather, I have been out and about roaming the streets with my camera. The urban parks are busy with families, pensioners and courting couples. No one knows how to relax like the good people of Shenyang; who else would sling a web of hammocks through the pinetum?

I've also been complimenting their attendant toddlers. This summer many are dressed traditionally in red tabards or aprons; the rest wear pants like chaps with no backsides. The kids are all as fat as butter, and I notice that an increasing number of pre-teens are not just treated like little emperors but decked-out like them too, in vermillion silk pyjamas.

I am delighted to find that riding a bike in China helps me to bypass the cultural barrier of my intrinsic foreignness, if only for the moment. When you are cycling, you are forced to interact with the local people, and they with you. You become a person, albeit the sole representative of an alien civilisation, rather than an object of fleeting interest, just passing by

The way of the dragon

133

Bouncing bicycles

2003, West Java: As with each and every birthday since his first, we bought Samuel a new bike for the 5th anniversary of his arrival in this world. He loves it; it might weigh a ton, but it has dual suspension and 'V' brakes that actually work. We took him to the zoo last weekend. As long as the tigers remain behind bars, there are miles of safe paths there for tiny-tot freestyle. The afternoon was a revelation of hitherto unrecognized abilities.

The wee bugger displayed a terrifying competence in the arts of riding blind drop-offs, blind siding and blind optimism. So now we know what they get up to at Ayah's house. No doubt his friends JoJo and Kiri will want suspended bikes too.

The new bouncing bicycle cost slightly more than a five-minute bout with the chiropractor and somewhat less than his themed birthday cake. There is nothing remotely rational about globalization and the comparative economic worth of goods and services. The bike is a size smaller than the bike I bought him last year; so that's next year taken care of too, once I remove the now-redundant stabilisers.

I committed the mortal sin of wearing sandals to work last week. My right foot was so swollen that I couldn't get my shoes on. Sandals with socks? Yes, I'm afraid so. Samuel cut me up in the closing stages of our customary race to the foot of the stairs at bedtime. His little heels are now large enough to cause considerable discomfort when wedged between my toes.

After a time, I was obliged to visit the surgery. "*Doctor Frankie, my gout has flared up again and my big toe is killing me.*" We port-guzzling, red-nosed, Dickensian figures of fun become inured to this type of discomfort, but it really did hurt like hell. After the X-rays: "*Your uric acid levels are normal, but your big toe is broken; did you trip on a rock?*"

I have little talent as a raconteur as my post-modernist sense of humour pre-empts the punchlines. However, with my penchant for ludicrous self-inflicted injury I can still make folks laugh. And how they laughed – everyone knows Young Samuel at the Medical Centre. So, once again, the boot is on the other foot. Meanwhile, the unshod, broken one lies at stage centre, encased in a crude aluminium scaffolding. I am now equipped to kick six-inch nails through skirting boards.

Normally, the bionic bovver-boot would have been no more than a minor inconvenience. However, Samuel and I were due to join Alison in Brisbane, where she was attending a course at the university. Help came from an unexpected quarter.

I can offer rare and useful advice; if you own a pair of stiff-soled mountain bike shoes, you are in luck. I sawed-off Dr Frankie's ad hoc engineering and squeezed my pink and unprotected toes into my bike shoes. It's a magic solution if you ever break your feet; although next time I'll take the cleats off as the airport security scanner threw a fit.

New bike, 5th birthday, Jakarta, Indonesia.   Image - the Author

Larger-than-life

2002, Argyll: The Park Ranger pulls alongside in his tricked-out Mitsubishi 'Animal' 4X4. Scott and I have stopped for a moment to consult the map and confirm our route.

Your man delivers the expected broadside: *"It doesn't matter which way you go lads; you'll be coming back again the same way. We're building a new trail over the saddle to Loch Goil, but it isn't open yet, and there's no other way out."*

"Och, it's yourself Ranger," says I, before responding with the well-worn riposte. *"Don't you worry yourself, we're local"*.

....and then: *"We'll just shinny down the cliff face at the Carraig na Maraig gap."*

"Well," says he, *"the Mountain Rescue's been out every day this week and they could do with a wee rest."*

"No problem," says I. *"We'll give you a bell if we're needing them. And a...h, by the way, d'you know if that fixed rope is still there."*

Scott didn't say much, but then he didn't need to.

Wimples, pinafores and leather

2004, Sumatera: We are 'on tour' in North Sumatera. I spent the best part of two years here in the early nineties. Not much has changed. Our scheduled meeting with the Governor this morning was postponed. He was attending the opening of a flyover, one of the last infrastructure components to be completed under our old Asian Development Bank project.

You may wonder why a simple junction improvement justifies such pomp and circumstance. Well, 'all the president's men' were in town waving their red-and-black flags to jump the gun on the campaign period for the upcoming 2004 Election. Our hotel was awash with red blazers; and of course, the all-black-clad para-military thugs of the ruling party were there in numbers too.

But our team is just here to reschedule reservations before visiting the up-country market town of Pematang Siantar. Siantar is famous for the throaty roar of its iconic 500cc single-cylinder motorcycles. The becak-motor (sidecar taxis) were manufactured in the British Small Arms factory in the early 1950s, while I gurgled complicitly in a blue wooden cradle proudly brandishing my own small British arms.

The local people are very fond of BSA 500 motorbikes. That perhaps is an understatement. In fact, they like them so much that over half-a-century emissaries have scoured the Indonesian archipelago to bring each-and-every one of these machines back to a spiritual home in Siantar. Now, literally

hundreds of the iconic old bikes ply the rutted roads of Simalungun County.

The vintage BSAs are a rare enduring legacy of international development aid – 'good works' that normally sink without trace. A World Health Organisation project supplied the bikes for various rural health programmes shortly after Indonesia gained independence from the Dutch following WW2.

Through the fifties and early sixties, dauntless district nurses, wimples snapping to the wind of passage, terrorised the countryside. The girls were game and simply unforgettable, togged out in gauntlets, pinafores and leather, burning up sleepy villages, trailing plumes of dust and oestrogen.

No doubt the reality was more prosaic, with an apple-cheeked health visitor perched demurely, side-saddle, behind her scrawny factotum; but even side-saddle I have no doubts that the old 500 could do the business.

The ponderous farts of a 500cc bike boasting just 16bhp recall a simpler world of low technology and even lower expectations. Once a year, the longsuffering cyclo-curators take a holiday from the hackney trade and travel en masse, en famille to Lake Toba. It's not far, but the trip to the giant crater lake is uphill all the way and many don't make it.

Passing the convoy, we see gay families in their Sunday-best playing tag among the road-side scrub, while pop repairs the bike at the verge. The scene recalls the days when mechanic's overalls and bruised knuckles were de rigour for dads on such an outing, when the shadow of death had already begun to haunt the British motorcycle industry.

Absentee agribusiness flayed this great region of its natural ecology and overprinted vast estates of tobacco, oil palm and coffee. We pass through eternal rubber plantations, dried up and no longer economic but still fain to dribble. I know how it feels. Serried ranks of venerable old saps bow stiffly at the waist, Japanese style, to hail the rising sun and cock their skinny butts to the chilly draught of the west wind. Only the occasional snap of perished knicker elastic robs the kowtow of its intended dignity.

I used to ride here when we were preparing an integrated infrastructure development plan for Metro-Medan. This was during a brief period when I owned the firm in partnership, so the project drivers treated my bicycles with great care and something like divine reverence.

I carried an early Garmin GPS to explore the Sumatran jungle. It was an orange soft-jacketed instrument which resided reassuringly in my backpack. It belonged to Louis Berger, a firm we collaborated with from time to time. When I was both lost and exhausted, I could read off the latitude and longitude and plot a course home. Eat your heart out Strava users!

In the case of Hevea Brasiliensis, a lifetime in bondage presages an early death by a thousand cuts, like battery roosters. But not for all; a lucky few straighten their backs and live out their natural span. By and large, sylvan genotypes are unloved; but, when old rubber plantations are left to grow wild, they become something else. I like liberated rubber landscapes, glabrous contours clad in frail feral latex.

The Brunei Hash House Harriers often ran through overgrown plantations in Borneo, where the good people of the oil-rich state have long-since decided that they 'canna be arsed' with agri-business. After twenty or thirty years the industrial forest is absorbed in the diversity of natural regrowth.

Erasure is almost complete but for the fact that, once in a while, trees line up. This can happen on six points of the compass and is no help whatsoever when seeking a way out. But if we chance on a small clearing outstretched rubbernecks nod east. When sunlight dapples the forest floor, rubber ducks.

A Scout smiles and whistles

2004, Central Java: I am writing this letter at my desk in the Ibis Hotel in Yogyakarta. It is 3 a.m. and I would much rather be sleeping, to be honest. Unfortunately, outside my window a small drilling crew is auguring the carpark to augment an artesian well. It's a bit noisy to say the least.

Still, for the itinerant workers and becak (bicycle rickshaw) pilots who doss down on the adjacent pavement for a brief respite through the wee small hours, the spontaneous fountain is a welcome opportunity to wash and do their meagre laundry in clear fresh water.

It's impossible not to be moved by the punishing physical labours of rickshaw pilots. If you use them you see a man reduced to the status of a horse, and if you don't you deprive that same man of what is more than an honest living. They may shoot horses, but the becak business is ultimately lethal in itself.

The sappers finish work just in time for the call-to-prayer at 4.06. Agh! I thank God for my celebrated beneficence and historic religious tolerance. After all: "*A Scout smiles and whistles under all circumstances*". So said Baden-Powell.

Nevertheless, a religion which denies the value of a good night's sleep to infidels and condemns disciples to a lifetime on the graveyard watch remains a mystery to me. "*I believe the greatest asset a head of state can have is the ability to get a good night's sleep*". So said Harold Wilson.

Me too, Harold.

Liver-spotted old trouts

2004, West Java and Argyll: We are gliding along the smooth asphalt of the expressway, bound for the trailhead at Cimanggis. I sit behind my loyal driver, Pak Hamdani, bobsleigh-style. To my left, the Chevy Blazer's split seat-back is folded forward, extending the load-carrying area into the body-o'-the-kirk. My favourite bicycle lies coddled beside me.

It's Saturday morning, the first week in August and the epicentre of the Dry Season. It is later than I intended. The sun is already high and there is no shade. It's hot, hot, hot! I am poring over this month's edition of 'Seahorse' (a yacht racing magazine) oblivious, distracted. Even so, sparks of reflected sunlight begin to dance across my peripheral vision.

I am drawn to contemplate the glittering intricacy of a pierced and castellated Shimano XT rear block. It's a beautifully machined chunk of jewellery, fit to accessorise the clichéd sportswear of basket-case-balladeers, hip-hop stargazers and Addidaddled drug-dealers.

Last week it was just a cog in commonplace sports equipment. It was caked in a cruddy compound of road dust and red dirt bound-up with WD-40. It was filthy; so was the chain, so was the whole bike. The weekly transformation into showroom condition is the result of an hour's labour by my house-boy. Prapto takes great pride in his work.

In Scotland, things are very different, bicycles don't glitter, even in the hands of enthusiasts. There, perhaps once a week before retiring for sundowners, I parry the midges to poke around despairingly with a bucket of suds and the washing-up brush.

Usually, I don't achieve much, bar split knuckles and gratuitous insights into the tenacity of matter – especially sticky matter. So, after half an hour, gunge and grime are redistributed uniformly over me and the bike. Man and machine merge disconcertingly, spattered-to-match in the livery of liver-spotted old trouts. Though to be honest, as the years go by and sun-damage blossoms, this tenacious precipitate makes less and less difference.

There are many aspects of life in the heaving metropolis of Jakarta that I don't like very much; but cleanliness is next to godliness and this is a god-fearing society. I wish I could bring my practiced pit-crew back home with me on annual leave.

Yesterday:

"I want to learn to fight Dad."

"Samuel, people like us don't fight."

"What if bad guys come here with bombs? What are you going to do then? We need to be able to defend the family and our home."

Crikey!

My first instinct was to sign him up with the NRA's youth programme, but on reflection we shouldn't dismiss these concerns out of 'cold dead hand'. Global insecurity under the acid reign of Bush is now such that we can't hide it from the children, even little kids of Samuel's age.

So, we have decided to introduce him to the oriental arts of self-defence and conflict avoidance. He is now enrolled for a course of Tae-Kwon-Do classes and thus in line for new pyjamas (white belt, Desperate Dan).

Fashionable, yes, but wise? *"A vital point is a part of the body that, when attacked in the right way (force, angle, accuracy), can cause paralysis, unconsciousness or even death. Attacks to nerves can lead to nausea, headaches or worse"*. It seems that the body has about 280 vital points, or KeupSoh as the 'Taekwondons' call them.

'Kill Bill', right enough.

Becak taxi. Image - the Author

Endless pythons

2004, Great Wall of China and West Java: The Shanhaiguan defences were originally built ca.1381. These massive fortifications reveal their antiquity in a fascinating patchwork of repair and refurbishment. The wall is a giant canvas for a graphic record of war, revolutions, and innocent little earthquakes stretching across seven millennia.

From the battlements, on a clear day the Great Wall can be seen to snake across the vast expanse of the coastal plain, all the way from the heights of the Yanshan and Jiaoshan mountains in the west to its termination in the sea at Ninghai.

However, today the old reptile skulked into the haze just a few kilometres down the road in both directions. This brought to mind a recent bike ride in Cibubur. Bear with me here in matters of scale.

I brake sharply as a python slithers across the open trail. The trail is a clear three metres wide at this point, yet for a moment, neither the head nor the tail is visible. It's like a passing passenger train at the level crossing, as falciform patterns set up a mesmeric stroboscopic rhythm.

Reality, time and disbelief are simultaneously suspended. The temptation is certainly there to 'bunny-hop' the beast, but discretion prevails…. I am still staring at the track in the sand five minutes later to convince myself that it actually happened.

We followed the wall inland to Jiaoshan Mountain, to the section where it bestrides a seasonal river at Jiumenkou. Much is made of the good feng-shui occasioned by the intersection of these two elements, but in reality, the union is consummated for a few short weeks in June and even then, only if it rains.

The 'great consultant' visits the Great Wall. Image – Authors' collection

Sempiternity reigns

2004, Argyll and Hampshire: In Scotland, we braved the worst June for 40 years. Then we flew down to the south of England to endure the coldest, wettest, windiest start to July since records began. It was a month to suspend reality; to hunker down on the bike and head-butt the unseasonable downpours, gritting teeth literally through a rising spray of road-dirt. In this way, I methodically consumed a year's supply of Ultegra chains, rear clusters and brake blocks.

It was also a holiday to drink a lot of tea and plough my furlough through Britain's bloated Sunday press. Our wheelie-bin filled to overflow every week. Generating these volumes of debris, almost single-handed, engenders a tangible sense of guilt. Whatever happened to the radical environmentalism of the Aberdeen years and direct action? Well, in my defence I never throw away a bicycle; they are either passed on to friends or simply accumulate to become a 'collection'.

Thirty-five years of 'reduce, reuse, recycle' campaigns have achieved absolutely nothing; mega-trash is just one more element of our obtuse, selfish and ultimately unsustainable Western lifestyle. Who gives a shit? Here we are led by the ears, held firmly by the balls and, it seems, defiantly proud of it.

This trip home I finally opened my crates, shipped from the fledgling monocracy of Negara Brunei Darussalam back in 1989. The local papers were pressed into service in June of that year so, for much of the unpacking exercise, they provided

more interest than my enduringly foreign personal effects. Borneo Bulletins and Straits Times of that era recall rapidly disappearing post-colonial lifestyles, before globalization swept it away. It's all a bit sad really....

In Argyll, sempiternity reigns, although in Cowal of course it never 'reigns' but it pours. The local are somewhat bewildered to find themselves 'gentrified'. Argyll is enjoying an economic renaissance. I guess it is long overdue.

On the debit-side, Dunoon's narrow roads are choked with aggressively styled, oversized, late-model SUVs. However, on the credit-side, the new 'white settlers' from the 'deep south' have money to spend, and this time, thank God, it's £s and not US dollars.

The big increase in aggregate disposable income means that the Holy Loch is once again a splendid arena to showcase great yacht racing, providing twice-weekly entertainment for dedicated armchair sailors such as my-good-self.

Our house, 'Anchorage' is perfectly located; we are in the grandstand, and I am fortunate to have the best seat in the house. Feet up, binoculars to hand; on my right, a decent Chardonnay – nicely iced-down and not yet half-empty; on my left, a big bowl of oven-baked crisps; and we have my daughter Kathryn on call if one or the other runs out.

I didn't go sailing myself and stuck with the bike this holiday. I am now fitter that I have been since living in Lombok. It seems a shame to return to work and metamorphose back into a discontented commuter, perpetually ensnared in Jakarta's heroic traffic jams. Perhaps I should just retire now and get back on the bike.

Well, retirement may be out-of-the-question for me at the moment; but, for many friends back home, when the question was posed, it turned out to be rhetorical. These days, in Britain, very few people of my age seem to be working full-time in a career-type job. This is what is now termed a 'passive income generation strategy'. However, other than donating my body to science (a plan reviewed and immediately rejected on grounds of 'sustainability') I cannot see any opportunities in that line to support my family.

So, we return to work, though after such a long break I submit to the routine with great reluctance. Back in Jakarta, we squelched abroad looking for the dry season. It was not to be found. South-east Asia endured, first unseasonal floods, and then catastrophic inundation.

We spent our first weekend at home, away. After a short week in metropolitan Bedlam, we needed a break. When returning to Jakarta, it's as well to temper the shock of arrival with a couple of days somewhere else.

Out among the idyllic seascape of the Thousand Islands the air was like ambrosia: soft, yet fresh between sporadic rain squalls. Breathing in and out was fun in itself.

Arran, Scotland. Camera-phone image - the Author

An electrified cat on a hot tin roof

2004, West Java: With weeks of on-again off-again sickness, I haven't been out on the bike much. Now alas, the wet season is here once again, and even the shortest ride can become a glutinous, heart-bursting exercise. But before the rains came, pretty much everywhere was accessible. Out by Bojong, I had a fine old time chasing whirlwinds before the rains broke.

Dust devils are common in many other parts of the world, but less so here. The local model resembles a medium-sized electricity pylon, upside-down, whirling like a Dervish. The devils are silent until they come across something that shakes, rattles or rolls, then the din is quite alarming.

I tracked one through a small-holding where it menaced an electrified cat on a hot tin roof before stealing granny's split-crotch knickers from the clothesline, twirling them across open farmland in a showy exhibition of centripetal magic. The by-now-tumble-dried washing was finally dumped in the upper canopy of a small wood.

The whole scenario was weird and somehow otherworldly. It was an airless day and bloody hot. I wondered whether the beast mustered enough hedgehopping horsepower to host the ET experience; certainly, it demolished a lean-too outhouse with ease. I imagine that rather than loft me and the bike across the landscape in an elegant parabola, the flight might have led to a slightly more chaotic turn of events.

A euphemism for lousy

2005, Argyll: Where weather is concerned, 'changeable' is normally a euphemism for lousy. In Kilmun, however, weather-buffs and weathercocks both appreciate changeable weather as a uniquely invigorating sedentary pursuit. I could have sat in the sunlounge and done nothing else through the holiday but enjoy the live weather show.

Kilmun is a small village, but we have history. In 1827, David Napier's ground-breaking (literally, alas) steam carriage linked Holy Loch to Lock Eck on the 'road to the isles', then the eminent chemist Thomas Thomson died here, and we also have Elizabeth Blackwell, the first lady doctor qualified to practice in the Western World, at peace in the graveyard.

But, more pertinent in this context, is that Lewis Fry Richardson, the father of modern weather forecasting, enjoyed an active retirement in Kilmun. Richardson's algorithm took three weeks of wizardry to forecast the next six hours, so his work only became tenable with the advent of modern computers.

I cycled every day; indeed, now that a line has been drawn to include 'Anchorage' in a National Park, there is no excuse not to – albeit that we are still in the same place and it's the park that moved in and expanded to infiltrate Cowal.

However, while the weather at this time of year may be entertaining if outdoor exercise is on your agenda, it's also hell-bent on bedraggling and buggering-up your day. So, in these circumstances, it's necessary to keep a reasonable-sized hill between you and the weather. Cowal's geography allows us to blind-side west-coast downpours, hailstorms, equinoctial gales and random acts of God. Well, sometimes.

On the endless plains of Java, if you see a big black cloud bearing down on you it is reassuring to know that it's possible to outrun it. Not so in Scotland – the squalls lie in wait, or dog your heels and mow you down.

After the rain, Holy Loch, Scotland. Image - the Author

Stalagmite sprouts

2005, Liaoning: Overnight, I have been transported from plus 32°C to minus 15°C and my old frame's threadbare upholstery has been cruelly exposed. But the sun is shining, and it doesn't seem so bad. In truth, it's another beautiful day in Manchuria. And now, I am even striding about gallusly with my torso unbundled, revelling in the sharp sensation of drawing icy breath through tropicalised lungs.

They don't grit the streets here; I suppose the salt would freeze in any case. As a result, everything is coated in dirty ice, inches thick. Petrified splodges and streaks adorn vehicles and road-side buildings. The verges are stacked with high-tensile ice sculpture. Mr Freeze is in town. Where is that guy Batman when you need him?

When we were kids, we were enduringly fascinated by the prospect of a piddle in these temperatures. Does a stalagmite sprout from the ground and imperil your willie? This afternoon, had I resolved to conduct the experiment, I would have been thwarted. I struggled manfully all day with the baffling logistics of my new long-johns. They were installed back-to-front, as I discovered when I got back to the hotel.

And of course, the traffic slithers all over the place. No matter, the cautious padding about makes us all feel a lot safer. Our European Commission financed, 4x4-endowed margin-of-safety presents us as the innocent target for once, and not the delinquent projectile.

My bike is tucked away in the bowels of the carpark under the hotel until spring returns. I am reduced to imaginary rides. Cyclists of all persuasions are especially prone to take a tumble, but the guys on motorbikes take no chances. They slide along with their feet thrust ahead, like the front paws of a snowmobile, skating over the hardpack. Their pedal-powered kin are denied that option, and thus creep about apprehensively, astride lowered saddles, skating on partially deflated tyres.

I have acclimatised and now luxuriate in chill air, snugly-smugly feeling the cold less than many of the locals. I watch them clump into 'Mulligans Irish Bar' and battle stoically to get their kit off. It brings to mind the audition scene from the Full Monty. Barflies unwrap, layer by layer, before the open embrace of a hatcheck girl, steadily disappearing beneath the mound.

After so many years living in hot places, where there are only about half a dozen modes of dress, it's fascinating to see what strange and wonderful things people wear. Cloakrooms and hatcheck girls – they're neat too. Is China the last place in the universe to have hatcheck girls?

Hot couture: beneath it all, the middle-class girls-about-town are into thigh-high leather boots and fluffy cashmere halter-tops – like frustrated Iranian housewives, or at least how one might imagine…..

Beyond the stars and bars, ordinary people struggling in the face of grinding poverty are, as always, the most picturesque. Among the terminally disenfranchised, the 'look' this winter is very much 'Stalingrad Deserter'.

Wadded PLA-issue great-coats, tied up with string, are worn with the classic cartoon-hunter hat, furry ear-flaps akimbo. The style is accessorised with carbuncled jackboots, flared gauntlets and a 500cc colour-coordinated, ex-Peoples' Liberation Army, flat-twin combination-motorcycle.

Oh, and the final touch – a gappy grin, pierced by torrid jets of exhalation.

Freefalling: the temperature plunges, spiralling uncontrolled through ever more constricting arteries of darkness. Space thickens, congeals, and curdles. As time freezes, it slows down. Now, almost nothing stirs.

The measure of life has been precipitated into little more than a chill ambience. Outside, a glacial lacquer of black ice decks the past, the present and the future in polished ebony.

I am lightly clad; and so, with little effort, thread the labyrinth spun by viscous strands of time. But the bundled rush-hour crowd is caught mid-stride; overbalanced, faltering – they all look unsteady and bewildered.

Leading with my shoulders, I tread a finical path among this ossified throng. What consequences might contact between two such divers temporal dimensions bring? So, for the moment I am content to remain a blur, in the universe of the imperceptibly animated.

That last passage may have slipped into allegory. Even so, there is undoubtedly something entrancing, almost uncanny, about the way outdoor activities falter, and are then suspended, as an entire city is stranded, held fast in fields of ice.

Routines are deadlocked. Peering out of frosted windows, the natives of Shenyang chew on pencils, and ponder the impeded anatomy of their being. Trapped in a blind lead, beyond the reach of contemporary technology, they gradually succumb to lead poisoning, just like Franklin's Last Expedition.

Oh God, it's happening again.

Ok today, it's minus twenty something and for much of the city it's business as usual; so, the 'Narnian' land of Manchuria doesn't actually hibernate, but it does become lethargic to the point where it become hopelessly inefficient.

Franklin's tragic voyage of discovery remains a salutary lesson in relation to almost every aspect of pushing the edges of the envelope, without first addressing it. As the great Victorian explorer scratched his initials on an iceberg in the Bering Straits; he signed-off on the reflected celebrity of two centuries of ballsy but meaningless rambles east – in the other direction.

The most viable great-circle route to Asia is still the Northeast Passage via Novaya Zemla. This route offered other advantages over the west-about route. When the pack ice chomps your wooden-hulled enterprise pear-shaped, you can walk home to England, albeit via Moscow.

The Royal Navy has always thrown money at imperial problems. Franklin was an unabashed techno-junkie, in relentless pursuit of innovative technological fixes. His ships were the first real icebreakers; boats with steel-reinforced forefeet, massive locomotive tractor power and piped central-heating.

And of course, he went for a 'big finish' when he doubled his bets and staked the farm on success in a very bad year for ice navigation. That Anglo-Saxon spunk was showcased again, more than half a century later, when Scott explored the other end of the globe during an excursion on the Antarctic continent to tread the diametrical reaches of the Luddite scale.

But sadly, for Imperium Britannia, by the close of the great era of exploration, it was two dour Norwegians, Fridtjof Nansen and Roald Amundsen who perfected a step-by-step primer of autochthonous approaches to survival. In so doing, they quietly debunked the in-your-face drama of Victorian public-school boys fumbling gallantly in the Polar Regions.

Franklin's men could have sailed to the moon. But instead, the local Inuit community glimpsed them wander aimlessly along the beach of the Simpson Strait, watched them 'discover' the North-west Passage and eventually watched appalled as they began to eat each other.

Horror and confusion, hell and damnation: huddled in the lee of a windbreak of tinned food, the crew were subdued then overwhelmed by foreboding. It's a gruesome story, which fascinated me when I was a wee boy (and a closet 'polarbore'). Even now, the names of his ships – 'Erebus' and 'Terror' – strike the latter emotion into the hearts of literate children.

I'm not sure where this is going, but we'll continue anyway: When we were kids, new equipment was fascinating – boats and bits of boats, bikes and other gear. We'd play with it endlessly and test it to destruction. Now, when we are grown up, we just pull stuff out the box, strap it on and jump. There is a reason for this, and a reason why things actually do work today, well mostly.

Both reasons lead to the same depressing conclusion about the cocoon of modern life. The first concerns our immature craving for the illusion of risk. These days, style is everything, caution is scorned, and preparation is disparaged. The trick-cyclists who participate in the X-Games have to practice in secret. The second, paradoxically, concerns the absence of 'real' risk in our everyday lives no matter how reckless we are.

Work Units clearing snow in front of their offices.   Image - the Author

Dhaka rickshaw pilot, mending a puncture. Image - the Author

All along the Watchtower

2005, West Java: The dry season is here with the familiar clockwork of a big orange sun arcing overhead, pulsing zenithal power like a gratuitous boot in the solar plexus. The lush countryside of West Java has evaporated into a parched moonscape. It is Saturday. I rise as dawn breaks and set out without breakfast for my regular bike ride.

I leave enough time to get back to 'the pod' before things hot-up; and before celestial mechanics exact uniform retribution on Java cyclists and any boiler-suited, bowler-hatted Droogs who may still be out and about these days.

Starting my ride from Cimanggis, I seek out the shade, crisscrossing the marginal trails above sweltering floodplains of desiccating padi. As I grind up a cordon bluff, I see an elderly man hard at work on his vegetable plot. He is probably my senior by little more than decade, but he looks about a hundred years old. His skin hangs in lose wrinkles, ill-fitting, mottled and burnished like antique leather.

I am cycling slowly, so I have the time to watch him work. The inclination extends the moment too – it is quite a steep path. The old boy tends Mother Earth with bovine equanimity, but he struggles pitifully to pierce the withered scab of her flaky, sun-baked skin. When at last, he penetrates the topsoil, his fork breaks out and the divot turns to dust.

The old gentleman straightens up, shakes out his furled spine and raises his eyes from the worthless dirt of his ancestors

to the pitiless sun. The rains will return – in about five months. He doesn't look round as I pass close by.

The other day, I called in at Plaza Indonesia to collect new lenses for my Oakley Airframes; the third lenses with the same expensive gradient prescription – the glasses are sold without a hard case. But that, I suppose, is neither here nor there. There is, as they say, one born every minute – and I am seemingly bound to represent our sixty second cohort.

Of course, we don't just 'call in' anywhere these days; life is no longer that simple. Wherever you go in Jakarta, there are scary kids in cheap uniforms with big, dangerous looking guns. comforting, they're not. Despite current intelligence concerning possible terrorist activity in the city, the omnipresent, not to say highly intrusive, security measures have become a bit of a joke.

While Plaza Indonesia's deferential guards probed our car for weapons of mass-destruction, a soldier of the regular army stood by, playing air guitar on his M16, searching out incendiary riffs, missing in action. He didn't look up as I passed by either. 'All along the Watchtower', right enough.

Bamboo bridge, West Java, Indonesia. Image - the Author

Merlin Mountain Extra-lite. Image - Wolfgang Burghofer

Sad old blokes

2007, West Java: After several years of impressive self-discipline, I have bought another mountain-bike. On the basis of that extended lifecycle, I'll pass this one on to wee Samuel. The various bits and pieces arrived at the Jakarta bike shop from small workshops in California and specialist factories in France and Japan.

Many of these crazy-expensive parts came packaged for presentation, like expensive jewellery. Should I ever want to take it all apart again and store the component parts in my sock drawer, I'm well set up. Of course, they didn't all quite fit together first time, so it took months to build.

Never mind, the craftsmanship is simply awesome; and how about this? The manufacturer's logo is not a self-adhesive decal, or even a metal badge; it's directly engraved onto the head-tube. A double-butted titanium hard-tail bicycle, fabricated by Merlin Metalworks Inc, is an indulgence that only sad old blokes can afford. But shit, it's beautiful.

Merlin pioneered titanium mountain-bikes, oversized tube-sets, s-bend chain-stays and s-bend seat-stays. There is a big bike retailer in the UK called Merlin that markets 'own-brand' bikes. These merlin-branded budget bikes are excellent but mistake one for the real thing at your peril.

The components on the new bike aren't bad either: the fork crown and steerer tube are a one-piece carbon lay-up, the wheel rims are milled away to tinfoil between the spokes, the

jumbo cranks are hollow; the stem and the seat-post came in designer bags and the carbon bars cost more than a Halfords bike.

Even with disk brakes, we are looking at an all-up weight of about 9 kilograms, or a couple of bags of sugar. Surprisingly, the bike is worth the money. The acceleration is just awesome; and it's as compliant as a watch-spring. If mountain biking is your passion, life is too short to deny yourself one of these.

But the big challenge for careful collectors is the bearing-busting destiny of all this satin-finished artistry. The sweet Californian will be thrashed through gullies of sticky mud, over plains of penetrating dust, across rocks and rubble and even rivers, through scrub and forests. Trial by mire will, however, will have to wait; it looks like the good weather will be here for a while.

Postscript: The magic bicycle lasted almost two years. One evening my houseboy called me out to the garage. He was not his usual cheerful self. He showed me the bike which he had just released from its thick coating of hardened sludge. Prapto pointed to the four-way union at the top of the seat-tube with an 'honest, it wasn't me' expression.

The seat-tube was cracked; the top-tube was cracked; the seat stays were cracked – across welds and junctions. The bike was utterly, totally and completely wrecked. I eventually did get a new one; these bikes are guaranteed for life. But it took a year, and did I ever receive an apology or an explanation from Merlin Metalworks Inc? What do you think?

'Merlin Metalworks' have had their ups and down. The firm was established in 1986, sold to 'Saucony' in 1998 then bought by the 'American Bicycle Group' in 2000. Unfortunately, ABC owned 'Litespeed', a similar brand competing for MTB sales at a significantly lower price-point. Bike retailer 'Competitive Cycles' bought the now-neglected brand in 2011. The frames are now hand-made in the USA by 'Form Cycles', but the magic of indulgence, along with the engraved tubing has, perhaps, gone.

Six Giant bicycles

2008, West Java: It's been very muddy recently. The Merlin is extremely good in the mud, but it's a bit like driving a Porsche Cayenne off-road: you can do it and yes, it's designed for that, but please…. Splodging down the track, I met up with a small group of enthusiasts I see out on the trail from time to time. They were hanging out on the veranda of a small warung, foraging through prickly heaps of rambutan.

I took off my helmet and joined the feast. The boys are perennially fascinated by my bike and like to stroke it. It was observed that I'd changed from Kenda to Michelin tyres – obsessive or what?

Unlike most of the new-middle-class mountain-bikers in Cibubur, these lads don't have crazy-expensive bikes. I like that. Also unusual in this bastion of customisation and individuality, is that all their bikes are exactly the same – all black, 'Model T' style. They told me that shopped around, did some research and struck a deal for six Giant bicycles, and very tidy they are too. The only downside is that the money saved is now invested in cigarettes.

Today, we are 'holier than thou' about smoking. But it's as well to remember that, not so long ago, fit guys smoked in Britain; pubs and restaurants were fuggy and tinged with gold from floor to ceiling. This fug was referred to as 'atmosphere' and thought desirable by almost everyone, including non-smokers like myself.

Here are some facts about smoking in Indonesia. Our company once angled to relieve Philip Morris of some small part of their burden of guilt, by diverting some of a punitive EU court award to appropriate restitution programmes in Indonesia. This excellent proposal came to naught, but it was worth a shot.

Indonesia is one of the oldest producers of quality cigar tobacco in the world, with a leaf-growing history dating back to the late 1700s. Bizarrely, the cigarette mafia is the main legitimate business in the country – when assessed in terms of paying taxes fully and promptly.

In fact, it is the Government's largest source of revenue after oil, gas and timber. The tobacco industry is the second largest employer after the government service. Therefore, attempts to reduce consumption through restrictions and pricing policies are inevitably half-hearted or worse.

Here in Jakarta, Mayor Sutiyoso recently implemented a total ban on smoking in public places and offices. The legislation is similar to Ireland, Scotland and Singapore; and now belatedly proposed for guttural old England. Still, it will take some time for this libertarian city's smokers to get used to such an assault on their personal freedom, aka licence to kill.

In Indonesia, estimates of participation rates in this great 'participation sport' range from 50% to 85% for men, though significantly just 4% for women. I have always maintained that the women here are smarter than the men. These rates are as opposed to twenty-something percent for both sexes in Britain and the US. Even worse is that, today, the Indonesian Health Department, perhaps conservatively, estimates that 25% of ten-year-olds smoke.

But then, as the next story illustrates, even if you are slim, fit and healthy, eat well and have never smoked, the Grim Reaper still stalks your shadow.

Himmelfahrt, Austria. Image – Fritz Schwaiger

The ride to Heaven postponed

2008, Hampshire: We were at home in England, watching the Tour de France. It was the final 20 kilometres of the 6th Stage from Aigurande to Super Besse. I was packed and ready to fly to Austria next day, where I would join my cycling buddies for a long-anticipated Trans-Alps bike ride.

This was a wheeze hatched in the quixotic Land of Zog. Albania had only recently opened its doors to the outside world, and it was still a fascinating hotbed of totally weird shit. We were developing an integrated strategy for the management of the coastal zone.

During our final evening in Tirana, on the completion of the project, Steffen, Fritz and I celebrated by demolishing several litres of 'Beaujolais Nouveau'.

The red wine came in recycled two-litre Coke bottles – I don't know how many bottles, we weren't counting. This extraordinarily palatable, ruby-red concoction was a gift from the Manager of the 'Hotel Mediterrane' in Sarande – a talented amateur vintner and generous to a fault.

Now it is July 2008; we have exchanged countless e-mails; we have made detailed arrangements; the stage is set for an epic Alpine bike ride. The plan is to follow Uli Stanciu's Trans-Alps route No.10, the legendary Himmelfahrt, which lies to the west of the Brenner Pass and the Etsch Valley. The Himmelfahrt translates as the 'Ascension' in English, or the 'Ride to Heaven' in bike-speak.

But something is not right here. I begin to slump into the armchair. I experience a weird, other-worldly feeling of being physically drawn deeper and deeper into the seat cushions. At the same time, I am drowning beneath a rising tide of overwhelming fatigue and looking down on myself. For a brief moment, there is a crushing sense of foreboding – and then the lights go out.

I was just switched off; no blinding light; no sequel to my brief out-of-body experience. In these circumstances, I understand that my soul is hanging around to see what happens next and a heavenly ascension is unlikely.

Christian mythology is centred on the Resurrection which elevated Christ beyond the visible heavens, to the mythical dwelling-place of God. Jesus got to sit at the right hand of his father – hence the term 'right-hand man'.

Since the much heralded Second Coming has yet to transpire, that chair has presumably remained occupied ever since. But, no matter, I try to be my own man and, not to sound ungrateful, but this was not the 'Himmelfahrt' I had planned.

I awaken to find myself strapped to a gurney, bouncing backwards through the Hampshire countryside in an acid-green spaceship. I am bound-up in a tangle of tubes, wires and straps. I have never felt so powerless. But I am resigned; I am strapped in and we are going to the moon in bondage. Heaven can wait!

Next day dawns and I find myself in a hospital bed, seemingly delusional, as I am still determined to get to Austria. Fritz calls from Innsbruck and tells me that the weather forecast is bad, with the snowline down to 1,500 metres. Since our route includes cols at almost 3,000 metres, a delay now seems inevitable. For me, this is good news.

I tell Fritz that, in that case, I'll be a day late; and, if the guys are happy to risk the company of an incipient epileptic,

I'm up for it. Dr Roberts says that there is a 50/50 chance that I will never have another attack. But first I have to get out of here, and that is suddenly not so easy.

With the epilepsy diagnosis I'd been delighted. "*Well thank God; at least it isn't my heart!*" Thus, I have no idea why I've been dispatched to some sort of intensive care unit. There are about half-a-dozen of us interned over the long weekend in a state of complete ignorance. Mysteriously, there are no more tests; and there is no more information.

I am now very disappointed; during a public conversation with my new mate Colin across the ward I question our custody and boast that I am the fittest person in this dammed hospital, doctors and nurses included! The effect is amazing; I have defiled the 'sacrament of institutional care'. There is a moment of absolute silence followed by a collective snort of derision that rattles the windows.

Though lodged beneath the masthead of a Specialist Cardiac Unit and wired into 12-point, 24hr ECG machines, we unhappy band of detainees (in orange institutional pyjamas, like the inmates of Guantanamo) cling to the farthest boundaries of reasonable doubt.

We continue to believe that this is all just precautionary. After all, in my case for example, didn't the good doctor say that my blood-test was in all likelihood a red herring? This is the longest of long weekends. Even with two full days devoted to the task, I still can't finish the blood Sunday papers. I need to get out of here.

There is a major down-side to being wired-up and plumbed-in that only becomes evident when night falls. After 'lights out', we stretch out, flat on our backs. So, as you can imagine, it's like the monthly muster of the Parramatta Chapter of the Harley Davidson Club at the Hog's Breath Café.

Gentlemen start your engines.

Doctor-like presences ghost by, but no one comes in until Monday morning, when a helpful lass called Lyn stops by my bedside to talk turkey. The pharmacologist calls by too and prescribes an arsenal of drugs to supplement the massive quantities of blood-thinner, still pumping steadily into my yellow and purple nether regions.

It's the middle of the night. I can't sleep and decide to smarten myself up in case I am incinerated along with all the rest of the hospital's hazardous waste. At the moment, I look like a hobo and no doubt smell like one too. I borrow a razor and drag my IV hook-up to the bathroom. It takes an age, but I return to bed confident that, when tomorrow dawns, I will now look like someone worth investing time and money into.

Next morning, the effect is not quite as intended. I glance down and see that the razor has not been wielded with the expertise I imagined; a litre of drug-emboldened blood has escaped and run down my chest like a curtain. I am now a bit part player in the Amityville Horror.

It's Wednesday, six days since the heart attack – for that is what it was; and the heart doctors, who I now know generally take their weekends off, have scotched the epilepsy story. The situation has, in fact, been crystal clear since last Friday when the test results came through.

I've no idea what was gained by delaying the delivery of this bad news. Rather than being happy to be in the best possible place for a man with his lease-on-life under negotiation, I have sulked over a missed a bike ride.

Major Bumsore

2008, West Java and Borneo: The first jokes I remember hearing as a child in the playground at Rashfield School were mostly spoof book titles and, as five-year olds, they just blew us away. The bogus books that come to mind, as I sit sideways on an extra cushion, included the apposite 'Ten Years in the Saddle' by Major Bumsore, and 'Twenty Years in the Saddle' by R. Stornoway.

My body is falling apart; not just (as long since) universal wear and tear, reduced reach and the painful residuum of cumulative injuries, but literally falling apart. It's winter in Scotland. I'm out on the bike suddenly aware that it gets dark early in the north. Inevitably it begins to rain, lightly at first, then torrentially. I turn my ankle. It grows dark and the trail becomes slippery and everything suddenly is very difficult.

I am brought to an abrupt halt by something-not-immediately-obvious thrashing the paint off the frame. I discover a four-inch nail pierced through my rear tyre – in one side and out the other like the palang penis jewellery sported by Borneo long-house Romeos.

Tom Harrisson, then with Oxford University, was said to have had his penis pierced on an anthropological expedition to Borneo before WW2. Harrisson restored head-hunting during the war, targeting the Japanese military, but he is perhaps best-known for his seminal contribution to the ground-breaking 'Mass-Observation' study into the everyday lives of ordinary people in Britain (1937-1952, revived in 1981 and still extant).

A wealth of social data was compiled and analysed and a whole new field of academic research was created. But then the MO programme was commandeered by the British government to manipulate the mood-swings of the wartime population, An unhappy Harrisson jumped ship and joined the army in 1941, volunteering for Borneo.

Lieutenant Harrisson's commitment to local culture paid dividends during the Japanese-occupation of Borneo. While he may have exceeded his brief by reauthorizing head-hunting for the duration of war, the impact was immediate and effective. Even today, long-houses display oriental shrunken heads, eye-sockets peering through the characteristic 1930s wire-framed specs of the short-sighted senshi.

Digressing is easy; resuming on topic is more difficult. No matter let's proceed. So, my bike ride that afternoon was not much fun, but that was not in itself unusual. However, when I finally got back to the car, I became aware that I wasn't just cold wet and tired, my bum was on fire.

When you cycle regularly, as I do, your backside becomes leathery or, more accurately, substantially inured to bruises, damage and discomfort. But yesterday, the skin just abraded right through to the meat; I'd ripped the arse out of my bum, like a wane rips the arse out of his breeks!

Alison thinks it may be the drug regime. Perhaps my skin is no longer waterproof? I bruise easily too – is the blood just seeping through? Some of the pharmaceutical datasheets cite an increased risk of haemorrhage, so who knows?

We will go back to England again for Christmas this year; countdown – two weeks to go. I need a check-up and we all need a break. Back home, it seems to be incredibly cold, even crystalline at the moment, but no doubt it'll warm up and become grey and slushy by the time we get there.

The old pump

2009, Hampshire: Six months later: The old pump is now rather chewed over with some more stents added. What else can you expect when your heart's perpetually in your mouth. I seemed to be muddling through an eternal rehabilitation as the latest hospital stay dragged on.

Then on release, my much-abused black-and-purple groin limited me to Mickey Mouse bike rides and very moderate drinking. Of course, it could have been worse, much worse – but then that doesn't actually make it much, much better, does it?

"Let us honour if we can
the vertical man
Though we value none
but the horizontal one."

Two months later: We go mountain-biking as a family so perhaps things are returning to normal? I am back to riding most days, alternating the road-bike and the mountain-bike. I have to say I now love it more than anything. There are some changes; these days I have an integrated GPS and heart rate monitor on the bars – which I have long since stopped looking at.

Anyway, I'm still here; and bloody happy about it to boot!

Dangerous dog acts

2010, Hampshire: These days I get more and more pissed off with people who keep dangerous dogs. What's going on? The dog-loving Anglo Saxons seem to have a blind spot on this subject, with all pooches given the benefit of the doubt – even those unambiguously bred to be intimidating, aggressive and able to exert the 'desirable' jaw-lock vice-grip of all well-bred attack-dogs.

I had an encounter with an extremely unpleasant dog on the trail a few weeks ago. I came across the owners first (hatchet-faced, bleached-blond mother and delinquent youth in shell-suit) who said, *"Look out for our dog he has a thing about cyclists"*. Then, on down the trail, I encountered the animal in question, which promptly went berserk and grabbed my foot. Fortunately, it was cold, so I had neoprene over-booties on.

I leapt off and put the bike between me and the dog, as is my usual practice, while the owner grudgingly called the brute off. I said *"Look, it just unacceptable to have a dog with 'a thing about cyclists', you need to keep it under control."* The immediate retort was a flood of obscenities. My stunned response was pathetic at best. The incident ruined my day.

Almost every ride along the byways and bridleways of Hampshire is a pleasure, but I did once have highly unpleasant experience with a feral farm labourer. I was on my road-bike; the road was single-track asphalt and some sod had accidentally made a real mess of it with an overloaded trailer, or perhaps just

173

held the laws that govern the use of agricultural vehicles on public roads with contempt.

No matter; coming along towards me is the culprit; one of these enormous Tonka-Toy tractors which now wreak havoc in rural England. Most farm-folks know the difference between a mountain-bike and a road-bike and leave you space to stay on the road and out of the splodge, in fact just about all the farm-folks in Hampshire for the 22 years leading up until this point.

Tractor man forced me off the road, for which I thanked him sarcastically. Then things turned nasty. His great machine shuddered to a halt and reversed back, blocking me in a triangle bounded by the barbed-wire fence, his tractor and the trailer.

Suffice to say I was very scared indeed and did what I had to do to escape. No bland police complaint could convey the sheer menace of that grotesque belligerent. But I hold a slim hope that one-day natural justice will prevail, and he will drive his monster tractor into the Fires of Hell.

Micheldever, Hampshire, England. Image - the Author

The Pfundererjoch. Image - the Author

Descending the Pfundererjoch, Italy. Image - the Author

A rare, ridable Alpine climb. Image - Steffen Brogger-Jensen

Dynamite Trails

2011, Austria and Italy: My heart attack was an event that arrived completely out of the blue and wrecked the comfortable complacency of an otherwise privileged life. Across a lost weekend of abject ignorance, my doctors played golf and I suspended reality, with a delusional attempt to discharge myself from hospital and join the lads in Austria for a crack at the legendary 'Himmelfahrt' or 'Ride to Heaven'.

Well, that was then, and this is now. I was given a second chance at life, and so now I also got a second chance to cycle off-road across the Alps, north to south by way of the epic, high-mountain passes. On this occasion, the bots had proposed Trans-Alps route No.8, the 'Dynamite Trails', which lies to the east of the Brenner Pass.

The 'Dynamite Trails' link up old military roads which were constructed to access opposing gun emplacements during the long and pointless years of mountain warfare that ran as a sideshow through WW1 and WW2. As in Kashmir today, there was no way either side could prevail in such an Alpine conflict.

The Italians had one spectacular success during the First World War; although like every life lost in the Alps, it affected the course of the conflict not one whit. They tunnelled under an Austrian hill-top garrison and placed 33,000kg of TNT deep in the heart of the mountain. Then they blew the whole god-dammed peak off. The Lagazuoi galleries remain today as a shortcut to the blasted summit, but that is for another trip.

Today, the crumbling remains of the old military roads are challenging in the extreme. They were never intended to provide a trans-Alpine through-route, let alone a cycleway for middle-aged mountain-bikers. They sidestep back and forth in search of inaccessible strategic cols and there they stop, leaving the vertiginous 21st century traveller to find his own way down.

Sometimes it's easy and sometimes it isn't. The tracks are strewn with rubble and the gradients are remorselessly steep. And where the access is driven from the south, the scenario is reversed; it's one step forward and two steps back and the temptation to abandon the bike is overcome only by the knowledge that the ride down the other side will be epic.

I booked a flight to Innsbruck and Fritz booked me a bike. I had no intension of risking my own little piece of Californian artistry on this occasion. Then for two months I trained to the point of exhaustion five days a week. I boarded the plane as well-prepared as I could be and crossed my fingers.

Fritz had picked out a good-quality, dual-suspension bike at the 'i-bike' shop in Innsbruck. But when he called them on the day that I was due to arrive, they told him that they had some good and some bad news. The rental bike he had reserved had just been stolen from its exhibition stand in front of the shop. That was the bad news. But and this was the good news, they had ordered a new replacement which was guaranteed to arrive that day.

I had considerable reservations when I actually saw the bike in question. The 'Scot Genius' model of that era was one of a small number of bikes recommended for Trans-Alps tours at that time. It was heavily down-hill orientated with huge knobbly tyres, long-travel dual-suspension, a complex triple-damper system controlled from the bars, and 30-odd gears. It looked 'fit for purpose', but it was built like a tank.

We swopped the saddle and pedals for my own rather lighter titanium components and decided to leave all the factory pre-sets alone. As his predecessor had gone walkabout I asked about insurance on the 'boy genius'. No problem I was told, if you lose it its €3,500 less the week's rental. As Fritz had signed the guarantee, I thought that was ok.

Fritz owns an engineering consultancy in Innsbruck and his partner Erika works in the Mayor's office. They live in Axams, a small satellite-town 12 kilometres up the valley, in a traditional Austrian house which is tall and narrow with four storeys, like a lighthouse. I was installed in a small bedroom on the top floor and made welcome with the first in a sequence of special meals and special toasts which marked every event, no matter how minor, during my stay.

The next day, Fritz took the morning off. We both we shook off a mild hangover and set out to test my new equipment. Fritz suggested that there was no point in riding light, if I was to learn anything about my fitness, or the handling of the bike under load. He surcharged my daysack with two two-litre soda bottles to be returned unopened, or 4kg of useless dead-weight. I am still not sure if I should thank him for this or not.

We rode the Birgitz Alm, then the Götzner Alm and finally the Muterrer Alm; for total of four hours 'moderate' exertion and 1,470 meters climbed, before the rain finally caught us. I finished the ride with my buttocks killing me and convinced that the bike was a disaster.

It was like pedalling a dump-truck and the downhill-specific geometry was completely wrong for climbing; I was perpetually slipping off the back. I spent the afternoon sightseeing in Innsbruck, but spectre of the unrideable monster bike clouded my afternoon.

Next morning, I 'slammed' the stem and removed the spacers to drop the bars, then repositioned the saddle to rotate my body forwards and down into a more familiar road-bike-like position. I rode up the Fotscher valley to the snowline at 2,000 metres. At last, we were getting somewhere; but getting there had definitely done some damage to my scrawny old backside.

That evening, after more Austrian drinking rituals, we weighed the bikes: Wolfgang's and Fritz's hardtails came in at just over 13kg and mine was 14.4kg. Since I was giving away quite a few years to these guys, this wasn't exactly good news; especially when we weighted the rucksacks against the target weight of 6kg and I found the best part of another surplus kilo on my shoulders. Happy on Schnapps, I'd let the lads persuade me to pack all the 'what-if' gubbins they'd doubtless be leaving behind.

Day 1, Saturday: Axams to Enzian Hütte, 60km, 1,746 metres climbed. The weather forecast was not great. Erika's mobile phone buzzed with a thunderstorm warning from her insurance company. The clouds hung low over the valley obscuring the tops, but there was no rain. We had an early breakfast then set up the electronic road-book device on Wolfgang's bike.

As we got ready to leave the rain started and the apparently soluble Austrians began to extrapolate trouble at the Brenner Pass. We brewed more coffee while I made the case for setting out into conditions that I knew nothing about. Coffee over, the rain stopped, and Wolfgang suddenly decided that it was a 'go'.

We rolled out of Axams and rattled down to Gärberbach and then started on our first climb of 500 metres to Patsch. We then continued along the old Roman road through the Wiptal to the Brenner Pass on still-fresh legs, swiftly adding another 700 metres of climbing to the morning's tally.

The Brenner Pass is narrow and there is just one way over it. That lunchtime, a motorway, a railway and three middle-aged mountain-bikers shared the pass. This was to be the only section of our trip on a main road. I understand that a 55km tunnel is planned to take the railway underneath the Brenner; it will be the longest rail-tunnel in the world, pipping the current record-holder in Japan by a couple of kilometres.

Half an hour before reaching the pass, the rain set in, so we arrived at the border-post cold and a little bit damp. Fritz made a beeline for a small cafe and ordered Coca Cola, soda and apfelstrudel, the staple diet of the Austro-Hungarian Empire, apparently.

We sat down to wait for the weather to clear, but the rain didn't stop. Snug and dry in my Gore-Tex, I argued the 'Albion precedent'. I told my colleagues they were thoroughly soaked already, and we could be waiting in this coffee shop forever.

So, we set out into the deluge. It was immediately clear that we wouldn't be able to make it over the Schlüseljoch that afternoon as planned, but we did think we could get as far as the Enzian-hütte at 1,894m. The electronic roadbook flagged-up the turn-off and we left the main road with some relief.

As this turn-off was first unnoticed, and then unlikely, it was clear that the roadbook was a bit of kit worth carrying. A 550-metre climb on good forest tracks took us to the hut, where we arrived after about an hour, wet through and shivering. We locked the bikes together on the veranda and scuttled into the convivial warmth of the Enzian-hütte.

The owner welcomed us and allowed us to dry our gear over the radiators in the dining room. The steaming kit made a special contribution to the atmosphere of a local family's birthday party at the long trestle table later that evening. We took a 4-bed room with one double and two bunk beds.

I bagged the top bunk, since my brother, Norman, always denied me access to that coveted spot at home when we were wee boys. It wasn't such a brilliant score at 3 o' clock in the morning, however, when I had to clamber down and go to the loo in the dark, fearful of breaking my neck.

Daniel Schwegler, the hut owner, has a thing about Canada. A Canadian flag flies proudly out front, and the restaurant is decorated with North American hunting trophies and a full-size Canadian bear skin. However, a subsequent internet search reveals that Daniel received his war wounds chasing stray sheep on the slippery slopes near-by.

Warm and dry, we downed a couple of shandies, known as 'radlers' in these parts (translates literally as 'biker'), and scoffed noodle-soup and spaghetti, while outside the driving rain turned into a blizzard, the landscape disappeared under a blanket of snow and visibility dropped to 20 meters. We had certainly timed our arrival to a T.

The Austrians were a little concerned about tackling the Schüsseljoch the next day. But according to our new friend Daniel, the weather forecast was promising; it would be fine and sunny from mid-morning on. He looked at us and said, "*No problem, tough guys like you will make it*".

Day 2, Sunday: Enzian Hütte to Ellen, 69km, 2,537 metres climbed. Three guys sleeping in one room and no snoring. Fritz reckoned it was practically a miracle. We tumbled out of our bunks at 6.30 the next morning and, even more unbelievably, there was sunshine.

The snow was still there but melting rapidly. Happily, our clothes were dry, apart from Wolfgang's shoes. We set off at about eight, riding where possible, but also pushing quite a bit on a path that seemed more like a streambed, with the meltwater from last night's snow.

It was too cold for Fritz, for some reason wearing shorts this morning, to allow us to hang around and admire the scenery on Schüssel's 2,212-metre joch. We quickly bundled-up for the descent of Mussolini's military road – hewn to the col from the Italian lines to the south.

We had a fast and furious zigzag drop of 900 metres, all the way down to the floor of the Pfitscher valley. But the pleasure of whizzing down was tempered by the intimidating prospect of our next climb which remained constantly in view across the glacier-scoured landscape, the-2,568-metre Pfunderer Joch.

This first major descent was an eye-opener for me as I left the Austrian contingent picking their way down like pensioners in my wake. The up-to-now not-so-smart Genius was a revelation downhill and made suicidal downhill adventures a great buzz.

After following the Fussendrass in the Pfitscher valley, still buzzing, we stripped down to our base-layers, repacked and started immediately on the 1,200-metre Pfunderer Joch climb – the highest pass on the tour. As we took our first break at a convenient hairpin, four disgustingly fit young guys passed us looking completely fresh, clad in white jerseys, with white over-shoes and white-framed sunglasses. WTF?

Fritz and I pushed our bikes for a bit after the break, but Wolfgang´s pride sent him off like a rabbit after the 'white team'. He caught them after a kilometre and found out that they too were from Upper Austria; it was their first day en route and they were on shorter Trans-Alp route starting in Fussendrass.

It took us nearly 3 hours to reach the Pfunderer Joch. For me, the last hour was the worst hour of the whole trip. To say I was knackered would be an understatement. I was at my limit and obviously the weakest of the party.

I had clearly been fooling myself up until this point, and we had only just started. I couldn't imagine how I was going to

cross the Alps with aching arms and these useless leaden legs. If I had forgotten that my left knee and right hip were reconstructed, I had just been rudely reminded.

The only encouraging dimension was that my heart rate stayed firmly locked in at 130bpm to 135bpm during this exertion. When I am out on the road-bike I have the alarm set at 160 and from time to time it buzzes discouragingly on steep climbs, or when I am trying to burn-off someone younger than myself. In fact, throughout the entire trip to follow, my heart rate remained under control and the challenge was transporting oxygen to the muscles, not blood.

The last 100 metres to the col, kicking steps in the frozen snow, were a nightmare; I could hardly scramble up myself, let alone piggy-back the portly Genius. But of course, I got there eventually, dragging the bike one arm-span at a time, to find Wolfgang and Fritz at the trig point frolicking in the snowscape.

Though it was late June, the col was still covered with 10 metres of snow with a vertical snow wall on the far side. Well, if it had been vertical that would have been ok; but when we got to the point where we could look back up at it, we saw a massive cornice with a thought-provoking overhang.

During the Great War of 1914-18, 60,000 lives were lost to avalanches. Military engineers on both sides of the conflict learned to target overhanging cornices and dynamited gullies to precipitate ballistic rock-falls – this was much more effective than direct shelling of deeply entrenched Alpine troops.

The view from the top was predictably awesome but it was approaching lunchtime and we still had to find a way down. Disconcertingly, I could see no way down. This is when it's a good idea to have some experienced mountain-men on the team. Fritz was swiftly assigned to lead the rock climbing, or rather rock descending, detail.

He disappeared over the edge like a rat down a drainpipe, with his bike carelessly slung over his shoulder. The route was off a traverse to the left, too sheer for the snow to cling to. I watched very, very carefully where he put his feet.

The slopes below the rock-face were steep and snow-covered so we persuaded Wolfgang to have a crack at riding it while I took photos. Fritz took photos of me taking photos of Wolfgang. You may wonder how Fritz with his ruthlessly minimal backpack was able to produce a camera at this point. Well, coincidentally, the 'white team' breaking the trail ahead of us had just mislaid theirs'. We slithered and rolled down to below the snow line and immediately lost the trail.

This was another mission for the Scott Genius, so I dropped the saddle, flicked the suspension to long-travel mode and launched. I didn't completely abandon my mates though. I waited for them on the far side of a wide, braided stream to see how they coped – crossing without 'Scottish' waterproof socks.

Well, Fritz had taken my advice and made his own with two thin pairs of socks and a membrane of plastic carrier bags, but Wolfgang was now about to experience very wet and very cold feet for the rest of the day. Bike shoes are not waterproof like walking boots, so you really do need waterproof socks. I still can't believe that 'Sealskinz', developed in the swamps of Norfolk, haven't penetrated Austria, but you've got to take your advantages where you can.

I had a long wait at the Pfunderer Alm road-head before the hard-tail-equipped Austrians finally turned up, feet still dripping. On the gravel track, we regrouped more frequently as there was so much to see and stop and photograph. Fritz again proved his usefulness by clearing a way through a stubborn herd of very large cows and pointing out small hydro-power plants, only apparent to an engineer.

We reached Pfunders at about 2 p.m. and stopped for a typically late lunch of Coke and apfelstrudel. Lunch was to become progressively later in the day as the week progressed. It was Sunday and we shared the terrace with some visibly drunk Teutonic teenagers.

They were trying to learn the new Tyrolean anthem 'Dem Land Tirol die Treue' from a programme on their i-phones. I'm not exactly into white supremacy and rousing anthems in German sound slightly menacing to me, and not just to me it seemed. Fritz and Wolfgang were clearly uncomfortable too, so we didn't hang around.

The steep, winding asphalt road down to the Pustertal was fast and furious. After this endless descent of 1,800 metres, we reached Vintl in the Pustertal, which lies at just 700 metres above sea level; then we followed the River Rienz down to Mühlbach. One thing you can be sure of on a Trans-Alps, is that every time you go down, you'll have to go up again. So, we immediately started our next climb, a 1,000-metre ascent to the Rodenecker Alm and the Bannwald.

It was a hot, sunny, energy-sapping afternoon. We drank a lot of fluids, refilling our bottles at roadside streams, before we reached the shade of the Bannwald Weg, a gently rolling forest road at about 1,700 metres.

I was beginning to feel a bit better on the trail and no longer lagged behind. In fact, from this point on I felt stronger each day, while Fritz, who had been earning a living during the month leading up to our holiday, gradually became weaker. Well, apart from one glorious last-ditch effort, about which more later.

By this stage, I had also discovered that it was the low gears that were murdering my backside. I now know that if you push slightly higher gears, this 'unweights' your seat and you no longer have to clench the slippery slope of an inclined saddle with your buttocks. A revelation!

My improving condition did have a downside. I was the only member of the team with my GPS set to display heart rate rather than linked into Ulrich Stanciu's Trans-Alpine vision. So, when it was my turn to set the pace it was inevitable that, eventually, I would get a phone-call from a highly amused Austrian. I'd then have to retrace my wheel-tracks and return to some invisible turn-off, where the rest of 'Team Europe' were sunbathing by the trailside enjoying another over-the-counter pharmaceutical picnic.

Just before sunset we descended to Ellen, a picturesque little village, clustered around an impossibly tall church spire, which clings to the side of the mountain like a limpet. We stopped for the night at the Berggasthof Häusler, where we secured the last triple room. I was awarded the single bed and Wolfgang had to share with Fritz.

The restaurant terrace at Ellen gave us our first glimpse of the Dolomites, which boasted a spectacular view over the Pustertal Valley. This fine guesthouse was obviously a popular spot with German hill walkers, hence excellent food. The Trans-Alps bikers had Radlers, pancake soup and yet more pasta.

This evening, as every evening on the trip, I had the ritual of rebuilding my left knee: first, on with a heavy neoprene brace, by now helpfully impregnated with Deep Heat; then, legs up and wait for my turn in the shower; next, into the shower to soak the troublesome joint with water – as hot as I can stand it; onto the bed and 20 minutes of deep massage with my thumbs; next, rub in the Deep Heat; on with the brace again; and finally, two chairs for dinner and one leg up for the rest of the evening. In this way, miraculously, the swelling reduced each night, and I started each morning on brand new legs.

Day 3, Monday: Ellen to Kolfuschg, 65km, 2,381 metres climbed. Fritz complained bitterly about Wolfgang blowing in his ears and kneeing his ribcage. But I slept like a baby, and so it seems did Wolfgang.

After an excellent breakfast, we set out early for the Wieser Hof, then on through the picturesque Alpine villages of Onach, Wellschellen and Zwischenwasser to arrive at St. Vilgil in the Rautal before lunchtime. There was inevitably some climbing, but otherwise this was an easy trip on narrow, winding asphalt roads through beautiful 'chocolate box' countryside.

We bought cans of Coke and chocolate bars in a small supermarket and sat down to plan our route for the rest of the day. What happened next was reported in Fritz's account, where an apology was offered. I will take this opportunity to accept it.

This was the scene: we are standing astride our bikes in the town centre. After some considerable discussion in German, the paper maps are folded, and it appears that there is a consensus. Wolfgang turns right, following his roadbook and Fritz, following his GPS, turns left; and I am left alone at the junction without any explanation. Wolfgang stops eventually, and as he is still in sight and Fritz isn't, I mount up and ride down the hill to join him. After this we parked our trust in electronics and resorted to asking local people.

Finally, we found the right way out of St. Vilgil to engage the Ritjoch, a 750-meter climb starting out on asphalt which soon became a good gravel road. As Ulrich Stanciu slogged and plotted all eighteen of his Trans-Alps routes personally, and his roadbook indicates a long and fairly level section, we looked forward to a respite.

Well, that didn't happen. As Fritz observed: "*If one integrates all ups and downs over the total distance, then he is certainly right*".

189

Eventually we reached La Valle, a hillside village distinguished by an old church of which only the needle-like steeple remains.

Lunchtime was long-gone and the gasthof was closed, but we found a farmhouse which advertised bed and breakfast. Three huge dogs guarded the entrance, so we sent Fritz down to negotiate lunch. Success. The elderly farmer rose to the challenge and plied us with heaped plates of excellent home-made fare: ham, cheese and apple-juice.

Fritz kept the old guy entertained with a plan to install a 30-kW hydropower plant to tap the potential of his spring. But alas, to quote Fritz again: "*I hope he didn't order the turbine right after we left, as I had made a mistake in the decimals, he would only get 3-kW*". Our man reckoned it was ok as he hadn't charged professional fees for this gratuitous advice.

After a short climb out of the valley, we continued on a sandy track, cycling through the lovely Armentara meadows, with the spectacular Kreuzkofel mountain range filling the sky to our left. I was teased for taking so many photos; but it really was gorgeous, with this incredible limestone massif bursting from the forested lower slopes.

I do love Scotland, but this is landscape of a measurably higher order. The journey could have gone on forever as far as I was concerned, but eventually we arrived in Abtei and, after the usual covert discussions in German, selected the correct valley leading to the famous skiing resort of Corvara in the Alta Badia.

It was already mid-afternoon, so we decided to push on past Corvara to Kolfuschg, at the foot of the Grödner Joch, where we checked in at the appropriately named 'Sport Hotel' for some unaccustomed luxury. The ski-slope led right past my five-star bedroom window.

Apparently, we were the only guests. Since the hotel washing machine was too big for our miserable little pile of

Lycra rags, the hotel manager's mother agreed to do our laundry on private terms. Fritz collected the smelly bundle and took it down to the receptionist, while Wolfgang and I de-grimed upstairs. Fritz was nervous about consigning his brand new €120 Löffler cycling shorts to an unknown washerwoman. Remember, he was so fond of these shorts, that he even wore them in the snow. Frotz set to work and washed his new shorts himself, hanging them on the radiator to dry – about which, more later.

We had dinner with the Sella Mountain Group, a rock climbers' paradise, framed by the restaurant windows. These are some of the most famous mountains in the Dolomites, but the charming young Italian woman who served us radler and pasta had no idea what they were called. So much for the education of the ragazze.

Day 4, Tuesday: Kolfuschg to Obereggen, 73km, 2,098 metres climbed. Waking up at 4:30 am, Fritz checked his do-it-yourself laundry. The central heating was stone cold and his only cycling shorts and gloves were still soaking-wet. Some of us with heavier packs had two of each, for this very reason. Fritz moved to 'Plan B'. He wrapped the gear in his bath towel, set it out on the bed, lay on top and tried to sleep. Well, he never did get back to sleep but, in the morning, he informed us that he was back in business.

The first climb of the day started outside the hotel door; it was 550 metres up to the Grödner Joch at 2,121 metres. This climb is features in the 'Maratona dles Dolomites' roadbike race; but, unfortunately, it is also popular with fat motorbikers.

We set out early while the 'lard and leather' set were still packing in the Bratwurst for breakfast. Wolfgang was soon out ahead, as usual, followed at short distance by myself, at last, coming into better form. Fritz, having had little sleep perched on a wet rolled-up bath towel, brought up the rear.

Rough riding on the Pfunderer Joch, Italy. Image the Author

Descending the Schüsseljoch, Italy. Image the Author

Wolfgang and I breasted the pass in good shape. Ten minutes later and well-rested, we were much amused by Fritz's delayed arrival, exhausted and gasping for oxygen. In similar self-immolating spirit, Wolfgang persuaded an Italian pensioner to risk his life taking a picture of us from the middle of the road, as we posed proudly by the Grödner Joch sign.

Everyone cycling these hills takes pictures at the elevation signs, though the sight of lone cyclists on road-bikes 'bagging' the climb by photographing their pride-and-joy leaning against the post does provoke ungenerous 'sad anorak' comments.

Our friend Ulrich describes the single-track descent from the Grödner Jochh to Wolkenstein as 'challenging', and so it was. The narrow footpath was stepped with diagonal log drains. It was another job for the Genius. Fritz fell off but, fortunately, towards the uphill side.

Then followed a broad but extremely steep washed-out gravel section, where we all decided that discretion was the better part of valour, dug our heels in, and slithered down on foot. Of course, just then some Italian hikers, climbing uphill on all fours, wondered why we were not riding our bikes down.

From Wolkenstein, we continued along the Gröden valley to St. Christina. There, we started the next climb to Saltria, near the Seiser Alm, and continued to the Paso Duron, for a total climb of 700 meters.

The roadbook and the GPS again disagreed, so we asked a German hiker who confirmed the route. Arriving at a junction near a chairlift station described by our friend, we stopped for a drink and a Powerbar. Meanwhile, this same hiker caught up with us. We again followed his friendly advice instead of the roadbook but made tracks so as not to be caught again.

The Saltria plateau is scenic 'Sound of Music' country at about 1,600 metres elevation. We passed through and continued directly up towards Paso Duron. This trail is another old military

road; not too steep to ride, but too steep to ride continuously, even for 'young' Wolfgang. We caught up with a group of middle-aged cyclists from Vorarlberger, out and about making ambitious daytrips; after that we didn't feel so bad.

Wolfgang´s roadbook promised us a mountain hut just before the pass, so we planned to have lunch there. As it turned out, the hut was too far out of our way, but Wolfgang didn't realise this until I was off up the track and almost out of shouting distance. My 'energy-attack' and useless metres climbed kept the others entertained, if nothing else.

Arriving at the lofty Malknecht Joch, we sat down and enjoyed the view with another gruesome PowerBar for a lunch. The fairly technical hiking-trail morphed into a decent gravel road and, after the first couple of hundred metres descent, we were able to look around once more and take in the scenery. I was in my element until we reached the asphalt road leading down to Campitello di Fasa 700 meters below the pass, when the Kamikaze Austrian contingent came into their own.

After a while we stopped to regroup and wet-down the brakes, but the smoking pads just boiled off our attempts to cool them. Disk brakes have revolutionised this style of mountain-bike riding. Road race bikes, on the other hand, are still wedded to weight-saving calliper brakes and still get into all sorts of trouble on Alpine descents.

What happens sometimes on these long steep descents, where conditions are such that you have to feather the brakes all the way down, is that the rims overheat. This melts the glue holding the 'sew-up' tubular tyres onto the rim and the front tyre rolls off the rim at the next corner. An alternative worst-case scenario has the heat over-inflating the tyre until bursting point with a similar outcome.

Since this was written, disc brakes have become more acceptable on road-bikes and now even you author has one of these heretical devices, but there is still some resistance in the professional pelaton as they are slightly heavier.

The 15 kilometres from Campitello to Moena flew by as we cruised the length of a sweet bicycle track in the Val di Fasa, alongside the turbulent Avisio River. Using the GPS, we managed to navigate through Moena, without the usual road-book detours, to begin the third ascend of the day, a 600-meter climb to the Paso di Costalunga at 1,745 metres. Wolfgang proposed lunch at the Albergo, shown in the roadbook as just 100 metres into climb; but, inevitably, considering the road-book's record, the hut was closed; so, no lunch again.

Hard by the closed hostelry, an elderly Italian couple confirmed that this was indeed the forest road leading to the pass. The woman said the climb was a "*serious piece of work*", but her husband replied it would be no problem, as we were "*obviously well-trained guys*".

In comparison with our earlier adventures, the ascent to the col was straightforward and we could enjoy the countryside. The trail joined the main road at the summit, but long before we could see it, we picked up the roar of vastly overpowered motor bikes roaring up and down on the narrow winding asphalt.

When we arrived at the pass, the roadbook advised us to turn right, despite the fact, that we could see Albergo 200 metres up the road to our left. It was around 4.00 p.m, so we decided to ignore our friend Ulrich and went directly to the cafe for a delayed lunch. Fritz varied our diet by substituting huge slabs of extravagant chocolate cake for the apfelstrudel, but we stayed faithful to the Coke and soda.

The cake apparently rejuvenated Fritz's muscles but his brain fared less well; he missed the next exit leading to Oberegen. I saw the turn-off and hung back, which was revenge of a sort for earlier in the day. About a kilometre later he realised his mistake and peddled grumpily back up the hill. The forest road to Oberegen was simply a pleasure. This time Ulrich's roadbook was spot-on; the track was narrow, winding, gently undulating and great to ride.

Oberegen is another popular tourist centre colonised by the motorised biker tribe. Our trio cycled around on the point of

exhaustion looking for a place to stay. We enquired at a hopeful-looking Hotel Garni; they were full too, but the landlady sent us to the local forester's house next-door where they offered B&B, with basic accommodation in the basement.

Poor Wolfgang was again consigned to share a double bed with Fritz. We had another excellent dinner at the next-door Garni, where we sat next to a mixed group of Bavarians, also on a Stanciu mountain-bike tour.

One of the women told us they had enough of Urlich's madcap deviations across the mountains. Like us, they planned to go to Lago di Caldonazo the next day, but they had decided on a direct route along the valley, not via the Manghen Pass. Perhaps they made the right decision; tomorrow would turn out to be another tough day.

Day 5, Wednesday: Oberegen to Lago die Caldonazo, 92 kilometres, 2,026 metres climbed. There were no complaints about snoring next morning from either Fritz or Wolfgang. I guess they slept as soundly as I had. The weather remained fine. We had an early breakfast and were away before the Bavarian group surfaced. The first climb of the morning was a 600-metres slog up to the Reiter Joch at 1,996 metres.

The reward was a 1,000-metre downhill to Cavalese on asphalt, which saw the Austrians once more in suicidal mode as we shot through the Rosengarten Mountains and past the vast Latemar Ski Centre. It takes a lot of balls to enter these long avalanche tunnels without touching the brakes; balls, I have to admit I don't have.

The little town of Cavalese hit the headlines in February 1998, when a barnstorming American jet fighter pilot attempted to fly under cable-car wires and cut the cable. Twenty innocent holidaymakers died tragically in the accident.

We cycled through Cavalese and recharged for the last and longest climb of the tour: 1,200 metres to the Manghen Pass at

2,047 metres. By this point in the trip, I was belatedly catching on to the value of 'le dopage' in the sport of cycling. Fritz and Wolfgang had been scoffing nutritional pharmaceuticals like sweeties since we left Axams and telling jokes about the absent Steffen's naiveté in thinking he could cross the Alps on water and chocolate during their 2008 Himelfhart ride.

Fritz had given me free access to his stash before we left; but I knew these things were expensive and had just taken a small selection. I used them sparingly – mainly because they were so foul to the taste. A PowerBar, for example, needs a full bottle of water to get down if you are not to choke on it.

But the other two guys were adding powder to all their bottles and following a systematic and seemingly well-researched programme of quick-release tablets, slow-release gels and energy bars each day.

The stuff certainly does seem to work, but I can't see my way to look for the easy way out as part of a daily routine. My Scottish Presbyterian ethics hold pain and suffering in the highest regard. On the other hand, if I go again....

The Manghen Pass is another classic road-bike mountain which features from time to time in the Giro d'Italia. It took us three hours. Wolfgang led out and I followed, with Fritz struggling a bit today and bringing up the rear. We waited for each other every 400 metres of elevation, so there was plenty of time to rest, unless you were bringing up the rear.

For Fritz, with no respite; it was just a huge grind. But he didn't complain. As he said to me: "*it's never a matter of if I can do these climbs, just a question of when*".

We had some fun approaching the top, duelling with the road-bikes; and even passing the odd pensioner as they slowly expired on their immaculate Italian exotica – all the gear and full team colours, with the missus following slowly behind in the 'team support car'. It's a climb they will talk about in the cafés in the twilight of their retirement; assuming they don't drop dead on these sun-baked slopes.

At the top, the weather, which had been brilliant since the Enzian Hütte, began to turn. The cloud was closing in and the temperature was only a little above zero. We stopped at the summit café for a quick Coke and apfelstrudel in the usual company of fat motor-bikers and emaciated roadies, then wrapped up for the downhill and launched over the other side.

Wolfgang was now worried about the state of his brake-pads and Fritz's didn't seem much better. We were about to plummet 1,700 metres, so brakes would certainly have been useful but as I have noted before, Wolfgang and Fritz didn't seem to know where the levers were in any case.

Having left the Mangan Pass in the depths of 'winter', we arrived at Borgo in the Val Sugana in 'mid-summer'. The ambient temperature was now a full 30 degrees higher than the high mountain passes. We stopped in a vineyard, stripped down to short-sleeved cycle jerseys and soaked in the heat like a family of crocodiles on a mud-bank.

From here it was only 20 kilometres to Lago di Caldonazzo. There is a dedicated bike trail. It follows the nascent Brenta River which drains Caldonazzo, so there is a slight uphill gradient all the way. Fritz found new legs for this last push.

Unlike Wolfgang and myself, Fritz doesn't alternate days with a road-bike; and so, he knows nothing of the unwritten code de l'honneur of the peloton, the etiquette about taking turns on the front or the easy ride enjoyed by the much despised wheel suckers who tuck in behind.

So, Fritz towed us all the way to Lago di Caldonazzo. We averaged 25kph for this section and passed everything on the road. I guess we were fuelled by residual adrenaline.

With our clumsy Trans-Alps bikes and heavy kit, caked in mud and streaked with road grime, we elbowed our way onto the manicured asphalt of the bikepath like storm-troopers cutting in at the school dance. Then, as we ripped through the day trippers, we sighted an Italian guy, togged up in the latest Lycra – dressed to impress. He glanced behind at the ruffian grupetto and rashly upped his pace.

In a moment of juvenile enthusiasm, I said to Wolfgang: "*Let's burn him*". We pulled out from Fritz's slipstream, put the hammer down and we were gone. Lucky Fritz got to see the emotional body language of the stylish Italian. His first reaction was to fight back and chase us down. But after a few minutes of futile effort, he resorted to the dolce vita. Since no ragazza had seen him, I guess he could relax.

Fritz knows Caldonazzo well from previous visits, so we cycled up the lakeside to the Hotel Mezo Lago, where he had stayed before. It is halfway along the lake, right by the yacht club which was incongruously hosting the German National Championships for the Snipe class in Italian waters, and close to a camping site where Fritz's friends were on holiday. We arrived mid-afternoon. This was earlier than we had planned due to our dear leader's remarkable burst of energy on the bikepath along the banks of the Brenta.

Despite being a returning guest, Fritz got the bum's rush from 'Mrs. Mezo Lago'. While she gave me a nice lake-view double, despite the hotel seeming to be empty, the old dragon condemned Fritz and Wolfgang to share a bed in a small dark room at the back, overlooking the railway track. The benefits of courtesy and old age, I guess. As for Fritz and Wolfgang, it was lucky there were only two trains an hour and they could look forward to the prospect of 20 minutes of uninterrupted sleep.

After a shower, we went to the adjacent camp site and had our first beers in a week. The alcohol went directly to our brains and life became easy. Later Maria and her daughter Martina came over from the camping site and joined us in the hotel. It was a fine

evening with much vino della casa and many toasts to our strong legs and impressive feat.

Day 6, Thursday: Caldonazzo to Trento then on to Axams, 22km, 263 metres climbed. The planned swim in the lake was abandoned as it was too bloody cold. We washed our bikes to keep the Italian railways happy and set off directly, or as it turned out indirectly, for Trento.

Buying train tickets in Italy is an incredibly time-consuming exercise involving long, seemingly pointless conversations with chatty but irrelevant officials, the forging of what appeared to be lifelong friendships, and many expressive hand gestures.

Tickets secured, we retired for cappuccino, apfelstrudel and ice cream. Our original plan was to go by train from Trento to the Brenner Pass and then ride downhill to Axams.

But the weather finally broke and the rains set in before reaching the Brenner Pass. So, we completed the return journey to Innsbruck in comfort. That was until we arrived. We had to suit-up and cycle through the continuing downpour to Fritz's Innsbruck office. There, we dumped the bikes and recovered our host's flash new Audi Supersportwagen to arrive back in Axams in style, where a warm welcome was waiting.

Wolfgang's wife Anita had driven down to pick up Wolfgang and so she and Erika received us at the doorstep with specially made Scottish and Austrian flags and the first of many bottles of chilled Prosecco. It was another excuse for extravagant toasts and serial gluttony.

On Friday, we returned the Genius to i--bike. During the 8 days cycling, I climbed about 14,500 metres on the bike, nearly all off-road. No real damage done; and we reckoned the rental would just about cover new brake pads and new tyres. The bike had done sterling service, but I wasn't sad to see it go.

As a postscript, Anita, Erika, Fritz, Wolfgang and I hiked up the Fotscher Valley to the Potsdamer hut. Disaster! The famous

Potsdamer apfelstrudel was still in the oven. I was persuaded to sample a Tirroler Speckknödel (Tyrolean white-bread dumplings with bacon). This is gruesome dish that looks like naked brains in soup. It was a scene from the 'Return of the Living Dead' and guess I was lucky to eat it before it ate me.

Finally, on the day of my departure, we walked up through the Kalkkögel to the Adolf Pichler Hütte at 1,977 metres. I took Fritz's bike along so that I could bail out early and get back to Axams in time to catch the mid-day flight to England. The others would hike clean over the mountain to Milders and return to Innsbruck by train.

Snow angel glimpsed out of season. Image – Wolfgang Burghofer

Dolomite meadows, Italy. Image - the Author

Strade bianche, Dolomites, Italy. Image - the Author

Head-to-head, Italy. Image - the Author

Night-runners of Bengal

2011, Bangladesh: This evening we visited the British Aid Guest House – another time warp and another hazardous journey. Clad, perhaps ill-advisedly in black t-shirts, we quit the sanctuary of our small hotel and plunge into a warm and fuggy darkness that only a meerkat might savour.

As if on cue, the few visible lobby lights flicker and die as another power-cut takes out the entire street. And with that, navigation is reduced to its essence, tracking a spoor of leaking sewerage to the end of the road. But no matter, because its only at the main road junction, that our troubles really start.

In any other city, this tree-lined boulevard would be an attractive thoroughfare. Dhaka is different. The sidewalks have been obliterated; the space between the rank monsoon-drains and the broken carriageways is piled high with builders' rubble – garnished, inevitably, with stinking (aspiring new middle-class) household garbage.

The traffic everywhere in Asia is terrible; but here it seems almost malevolent, with noisy, bad-tempered car drivers choking on their own exhaust fumes. Still, at least they have lights and rounded edges. The real danger lurks alongside, between and sometimes, one assumes, underneath: rickshaws, unlit, in countless numbers, riding in close-packed formation – rippling metallically across interstitial space.

Only the roadside palm trees stand firm against this riptide. So, to a man, we dodge from palm to palm, line-astern in the

backwater. It just needs one last push. Sucking in our stomachs, we leave the relative safety of the last tree. Immediately, we find ourselves recast as organic shear-pins in a matrix of overlapping, gridlocked rickshaws.

What to do? What can you do? Close your eyes, take a deep breath and think of England? But no, as good consultants we have one last trick up our sleeves – suspend reality and resort to sleight of hand. It works. Miraculously, everything grinds to a halt with no harm done. And so, once again happily out of touch with the real world, we survive to tell the tale – though not before a final brush with a lethal web of sparking, low-slung power cables.

Welcome to the Bagha Club. I am, not immune to, and often thankful for, the life-affirming imbibition of a cold beer.

The style here is unreconstructed empire. On the ground floor, the dining room is outfitted with the very same rattan furniture and homely floral upholstery fabrics which blind-sighted the returning community of post-war colonials to an irrevocably changed subcontinent in 1946. Upstairs, the chairs and barstools might have been constructed by apprentice shuttering joiners.

In the intervening space, the stair-well is hung with framed albums sleeves from the seminal rockers of the 1970s. It reminded me of the World-Wide Helicopters Club in Borneo. A couple with young children were dining downstairs – I thought 'what a bloody awful place Dhaka must be for an English family when this decrepit old boozer is a good night out'.

Traffic is never so bad on a return trip, but we did have to bob and weave to negotiate a smouldering, spitting bonfire. Back at the hotel, Joe, more thick-skinned than we had previously suspected, noticed some new bullet holes in his breeks; the cinders had burnt clean through his trousers!

It is the week leading up to the Eid al-Adha public holiday when not much ever gets done. Our local partner's office is fortunately close by, so next morning Joe and I take a rickshaw over there and make plans to make the best use of our time. We arrange site-visits to get an idea of the physical form of the city and the lifestyles of people who live here.

Needless to say, it's mind-blowing. The Dhaka poverty rate is 45%; and then, when you realise that there are 15 million inhabitants here, well, for this privileged scion of Western culture, the struggle to survive is humbling.

Dhaka is perhaps the mega-city most at risk from climate change. It is also a city hell-bent on self-destruction. The surrounding wetlands are disappearing under a blanket of slurry pumped from the main rivers. No one knows how this vast land reclamation project will turn out.

What is certain is that the total capacity of the natural buffer zones within the river system is being dramatically reduced. So, when floods occur in the future, they will be more frequent, deeper and more destructive. And they will appear with less warning. With ongoing climate change, global weather patterns are becoming ever more erratic, and the formerly remote possibility of a devastating 100-year flood is set to become an annual event.

The actions of the big developers and government agencies are, of course, contrary to the city development plans. With the poachers and gamekeepers shacked-up in bed together, the scale of transgression is striking.

What makes all this worse is that the new wall-to-wall carpet of speculative real estate will only address the housing needs of a small minority of affluent Dhaka residents. For the 'poor', compensation is around 10% of real market value and for the 'landless very poor' there is less than nothing.

When I have the chance, I take photographs, which strike me later as an ambivalent essay on the marginalisation of a fragile riparian society. The urban environment is crushing, but there are beautiful people everywhere. There you go. Anyway, before we slit our wrists, we flag down a Bajaj and head down-town to the Sheraton for quick shot of socio-economic bandwidth.

In Bangladesh, the Bajaj three-wheel taxi, as it arrives from India, looks much like the familiar menace of urban roads in Indonesia. But here they add adrenaline to the ride by encasing the passenger compartment in a stout steel cage. The door clangs shut, and the driver rams an over-sized garden-gate latch bolt across to hold it there. Joe and I are clamped like a brace of pork chops in a barbeque grill. And off we go, with the world around us assigned to grid squares.

The close packing in traffic is by turns terrifying and awesome. A Bajaj is pointed in front and fat at the back; in fact, bar the lack of a tail it's a lot like a giant mechanical rat. Everyone knows this, so everyone cuts these little vehicles up with impunity. In some cities it's unwise to rest your elbow on the window frame but here a fingernail would be hazardous, as it becomes immediately clear why we are in a protective cage.

But then imagine the return trip in the dark: the noise is tremendous with the rattling of the cage, the tortured scream of an overstressed 2-stroke motor, road noise and a continuous cacophony of horns and claxons. Also, obvious now, is the function of the after-market tubular steel bumpers on the saloon cars – they are Bajaj brakes.

Next evening, we ventured abroad in the comparative safety of a bicycle rickshaw and took turns pedalling while our, understandably nervous, professional pilot perched in the back with the balance of our reclining neo-colonial piss-artists. So, we paid tribute to the 'Night-runners of Bengal'.

Stevenson's Rocket

2012, Bangladesh: In emerging democracies, the army is a mixed blessing and an institution that must be spoilt rotten. In Bangladesh, they need both toys and carrots-on-sticks to stay happy – to wit, arms down and feet up in the barracks. One lucrative diversion is the award of juicy public works contracts to the Core of Engineers.

It's more expensive than the typical competitive tender processes – but then again, in the context of the bigger picture, maybe it's not. We ventured into army-land to check out a notorious link road that cannot be completed as it 'cul-de-sacs' at the cantonment. This excursion freaked out Akbar, our normally happy-go-lucky driver.

Of course, we were merely asked to leave politely. But not before coming across a bunch of squaddies laying black-top with a totally brilliant piece of antediluvian kit. Sadly, the mad Macadam machine was pointing into the sun and I couldn't catch the open furnace and the colossal smoke plume together in the same frame.

Imagine Stevenson's Rocket on stilts, shooting sparks and belching black smoke, thick as toothpaste. And underneath, a pathetic little poop of glistening asphalt rattled onto the flatbed like a giant chocolate crispy.

But the best, the absolute killer, was that flat-bed waggon beneath the Rocket was a pedal-powered tricycle!

Bangladesh Armed Forces construction crew. Image - the Author

Dhaka rickshaw pilot. Image - the Author

Dhaka rickshaw passenger. Image - the Author

Demolition day

2012, Bangladesh: The day's demolition was carried out with the aid of a big yellow bulldozer and attended by a ragged squad of nervous day-labourers, sporting stylish red bandanas to differentiate them from the pressing crowd.

Of course, these evictions and demolitions are not always good clean fun, and anything from sporadic violence to riots must be anticipated. So, we were accompanied by a personal detail of eight armed police, culled from the assembled riot-squad, to safeguard against any possible misadventure.

I've had minders before, that comes with the territory, but I have to say that eight Bengal Bobbies, in shiny black plastic riot gear from the waist down, and their best number ones from the waist up, constituted an impressive honour guard.

The boys were friendly and courteous but armed to the teeth; totting Chinese-made Type-81 semi-automatic assault rifles, clutched casually by the pistol-grip, Rambo-style, metal stock folded back. I don't know what the locals thought of it, but I tell you that arsenal kept me in line.

However, all this super-cool, super-cop stuff took a slight knock when the real elite turned up. RAB, the Bangladesh 'Rapid Action Battalion', cruised by to make their presence felt and act as a further deterrent to anyone still looking to make it into Thursday's print-media.

So what; we already had a small army on-site. However, for the delectation of martial-style fashionistas, the RAB guys

certainly raised the ante. Immaculate black battledress, boots-that-fit and tailored black bandanas, Oakley shades and pirate earrings – killer-chic.

Back to the operation: even after the power company cut their illicit electricity supplies, the owners of the illegal buildings made no effort to comply with the removal order. Right up until the bulldozer gently laid its giant yellow bucket on the roof, they simply didn't believe it would happen.

Then, suddenly, it was all too real. The heads and shoulders of the assembled petty traders and drug-dealers dropped in unison. This, now grovelling, crew petitioned the magistrate for a little time to salvage their property and their belongings and, generously, they were given a brief reprieve.

In short order, whole buildings were disassembled and stacked high on a convoy of itinerant tricycles; no doubt to be reassembled just around the corner. Then the owners further down the street belatedly began to understand that this just wasn't going to be their day and frantically began to whistle-up even more tricycle-touts to help pull their shacks apart and salvage their lives.

Bicycles aren't middle-class toys in developing countries, they underpin society.

Under the harsh light of our 'international scrutiny', the magistrate bent over backwards to be fair, and so only that part of the various illegal buildings located within the road reserve was demolished. The owners of any residual illegal structure remaining outside the road reserve can now expect separate notices issued under a different clause of the act.

On the basis of what we saw, the enforcement action was a well-run process. However, each eviction is different and, depending on the level of physical resistance, conflict and latent violence is always bubbling just under the surface.

In an unrelated event, a confabulation of local mullahs, representing twelve Islamist Parties, called a general strike next morning. They are protesting the 'Innocence of Muslims' movie and the 'Charlie Hebdo' cartoons. The good people of Dhaka were incited to rise to this tainted bait and storm the US Embassy, among other satanic targets. So, the hotel went into full lockdown. Unfortunately, it was the day of my departure.

After a quick breakfast, I packed up and descended to the lobby to find the hotel minibus accessorised with large POLICE signs front and back and graced with an armed police detail. The security guards unchained the gate and we launched into almost empty streets. The trip, which normally takes an hour and a half, was over in just twenty minutes, Alhamdulillah!

Bangladesh flat-bed tricycle pilot. Image - the Author

The butcher's battle-axe

2012, Bangladesh: Pharmas all over the world are big on brazen bribes to encourage doctors to use their products. In this instance they had dreamt up a very special gift, a 2-foot-long chapatti (ceremonial cleaver) to spice up staid Dhaka surgery walls, normally the domain of prosaic framed diplomas. What balding, red-blooded medico could resist?

One pharmaceutical sales rep was riding his motorcycle through the university campus, with a loosely wrapped bundle of these butchers' battle-axes on the pillion, when he hit a bump. Fifty lethal weapons fell off and clattered across the road.

Two helpful young women rushed over to help him pick up the mock weaponry. Unfortunately, the girls sported teeshirts of allegiance to the BNP Student Faction. Even more unfortunately, members of the quarrelsome Awami League saw all this and jumped to conclusions, as they so often do with unpredictable consequences. These gung-ho vigilantes surrounded the battle-axe trio and called the police.

This was actually a famous stroke of luck since a more likely scenario is for the mob to set fire to the bike and kick the shit out of the rider and any vulnerable BNP bystanders. On this occasion, in short order, the hapless rep was handcuffed, arrested and then carted off to prison to be charged with arming and abetting a riot.

Fortunately, our rep was not without friends. He called his cousin Nazem, one of our professional counterparts here.

Nazem provided a stout character reference and, after a quick consultation with the shell-shocked pharmaceutical arms-dealer, scratched together the paltry funds required to secure bail.

Our somewhat chastened rep still has to attend court in a few weeks' time, however. As to the wider cleaver-culture, when you order a chapatti flatbread in a Bangladeshi restaurant after grumbling about the service, be careful what you ask for!

Restaurant, Bangladesh. Image - the Author

A hard life in Bangladesh. Image - the Author

I blame Bradley Wiggins

2012, Scotland: Summer in Argyll: The big events for Samuel were: bike rides to circumnavigate the islands of Bute and Arran; a back-and-forth challenge to Carrick Castle; and finally, a rubber dinghy expedition down the River Echaig. It wasn't a great summer weather-wise. Well, to be honest, it was dire, but by shuttling between Scotland and Hampshire, we had the best of it.

I had ridden round Bute for the first time on my first trip north of the summer, but that had been from the house and, at nearly 90 miles, it was not really a family-friendly excursion. So, we drove to the Colintraive Ferry with the mountain-bikes on back, left the car there and started our ride across then channel on the island. It was a beautiful day for a circum-perambulation.

We stopped first in Kames for an excellent café latté at the post office-cum pavement café. Then, over the hill to Ettrick Bay which was thronged with day-trippers. It's an endless sandy beach so we could still find a solitary spot to picnic happily, with Arran purple and massive on the horizon beyond a star-spangled sea. Back on the road, there was time for a puncture by Scalpse Bay and ice creams in Rothesay before the mad dash to the ferry.

The trip off-road to Carrick Castle was something I had long planned to do. It used to be a cross-country hike but now, thanks to some well-directed investment in cycle routes by the European Union, it's not only possible, it's a pleasure.

A new single-track link has been driven through to Carrick from the end of the forest road leading north from Ardentinny paralleling Loch Long. In common with other such initiatives in Cowal, no attempt has been made to 'dumb-down' the cycling challenge of circuitous lines and steep gradients which respect the contours of the landscape.

Samuel punctured tyres riding both my bike and his own and I broke my chain twice. Alison rediscovered some of her old single-track skills that used to impress me so much wandering abroad, among the foothills of the Java mountains.

Alan Bunyan was a well-liked water-sports instructor. Alan worked under Chris at the Scottish National Sailing Centre. He died in a tragic kitesurfing accident at Cumbrae a few years ago. His family and friends have created an annual 'Alan Bunyan Memorial Bike Ride' round Arran to honour his memory.

Samuel was especially keen to join the ride. I guess there is always something special about cycling round an island, but Arran is one of the best in this context, with 55 miles of good asphalt and a few good hills along the way. We dropped Alison off at the airport and got ourselves organized.

Samuel rode Alison's Marin with a set of semi-slicks, and I took my Look road-bike. The boy was the only member of the group riding a mountain-bike. He did well, taking his turn at the front, while Dawn, Chris and I brought up the rear. Arran was jumping with cyclists – there must have been more than two hundred bikes on the ferry, largely state-of-the-art carbon.

Certainly, it was a vast and colourful mob of Lycra-louts who massed on the jetty to board the ferry through the big bow doors. Perhaps reflecting on the 'bikes travel free' fare structure, a dour old seaman in charge of loading was heard to mutter: "*I blame Bradley Wiggins for all this nonsense*".

Merlin and bicycle sculpture, SDW, Hampshire. Image - the Author

Chalk and cheese

2013, England: For some years now, I had been looking at the South Downs Way (SDW) and wondering how to organise the logistics for a multi-day, one-way ride from Winchester to Eastbourne. However, this spring I have been cycling a bit more than usual in preparation for another testing Trans-Alps through Austria, Switzerland and Italy.

My marginally increased fitness seemed to offer a solution, albeit a rather brutal one for a sexagenarian cyclist beset by more chronic health defects than the English economy. Firstly, I realised that if I cycled from the trailhead in Alresford, rather than the King Alfred Statue in Winchester, I could join the SWD route at 'Mile 6' with 4.5 miles on the clock and plenty of opportunities to make good the 1.5-mile deficit; secondly, if I could complete the whole route in a single day it would simplify matters even more. It's only three times the distance and twice the climbing of a hard day in the Alps – what could go wrong?

The South Downs Way is a long-distance bridleway running the length of the rolling downs of southern England. The SDW lies within our newest National Park – 1,627 square kilometres of historic chalk downland designated in 2011. It is pretty special.

Even if you know the South well, this broad swath of upland is surprising. It feels vast and beautiful, unspoiled and mysterious. It was peopled with defensive agricultural settlements in prehistoric times. Intriguing earthworks bear witness to that era. These upland villages were abandoned when marauding went out of fashion, to enable a move down onto the more benign environments of the floodplains. You'll notice that in the self-effacing land of England 'downland' is 'upland'.

The SDW runs for 100 miles (161 kilometres) from Winchester in Hampshire to Eastbourne in East Sussex, with a claimed 13,620 ft (4,150 metres) of climbing. Something like 90% of the trail is off-road. It is said to be "*the toughest off-road ride in the UK*".

The Park Authority says that "*the time it takes to cycle the South Downs Way is hard to estimate as so much depends on your personal fitness and equipment. As a very rough guide, casual cyclists will take 3 to 4 days, regular off-road cyclists about 3, and the very fit cyclist looking for a challenge could do it in two. If you're capable of cycling 100 miles off road in just one day, then you'll know about it!*"

Inevitably, on this small uber-competitive island, various sporting events are held along the route, including the British Heart Foundation's annual 'Randonee' 100 mile mountain-bike race. Cyclists also compete over 35 and 60-mile courses to support heart-attack rehab programmes.

The fastest times for the full distance are reputed to be sub-8 hours, but most competitors take between 10 and 14 hours. The 100-mile Randonee is a Grade 5 route said to be "*suitable for only the most experienced, fit, skilful riders. Technicality: very difficult, with terrain suitable for expert riders only. Strenuousness: extremely strenuous- riders should be at peak fitness*".

Well to be honest, there are no really 'difficult' or dangerous technical sections – as in the rocky staircase descents of the Alps; although to be fair, maintaining traction while climbing steep, root-crossed, flint-strewn gullies isn't always exactly easy and is sometimes close to impossible. As for the 'strenuous', well I can't really argue with that.

Much of the route is on high chalk downland, with superb views from the open ridgeway sections, where the only indications of the trail are an arrow at the last field boundary, which might be a mile back. In some sections, there are a lot of those, and I'd estimate more than 100 gates have to be opened and closed – which hardly facilitates sub-eight-hour times.

I know nearby sections of the SDW well and include them regularly in circular rides from home, so I cycled the first 25 miles of the route in a 'there-and-back' ride to give me a head-start on the initial route-finding. Ominously I got lost; more ominously, I was too casual with rehydration and nutrition and I 'bonked' on the trail home, arriving back totally wasted.

No matter, thus admonished, preparations continued: I broke out my newly purchased 2013 Trans-Alps kit, fitted low-rolling resistance cross-country racing tyres to the Merlin, tuned the bike's XLM mechanicals to run like a sewing machine, tuned into the long-range weather forecast and set a date. Nothing was left to chance.....

One Wednesday in May, I rose at 5.00 am and, following a recommended big-ride diet, tucked into a big bowl of porridge, bananas, and yogurt. I used to hate porridge as a child – it sits in your stomach like brick until lunchtime; but, on this occasion, nervous energy burnt it up within the first ten miles.

I set off at six and followed the bridleway to meet up with the SDW near Cheesefoot Head. The north face of this hill is natural amphitheatre. It was the scene of a vast open-air boxing tournament organised by the US Army in 1944, featuring the great Joe Louis. Oh yes, and General Eisenhower also addressed the American troops here prior to D-Day.

I gradually warmed to my task on Beacon Hill and over Wheely Down. Old Winchester Hill followed at the small cost of a splodge of cowshit in the face. This hill is an SSSI crowned

by an Iron Age hill fort but, as I pass it every week on my regular road-bike circuits, it didn't get so much as a glance this morning.

Then downhill past the still out-of-season lake-side cafe at Meon Springs, before zigzagging across open fields to the base of Salt Hill, which is climbed via a steep gravel chute. Most cyclists walk up this one, so I was rather pleased with myself as I cleaned it without too much effort in the middle ring.

This smugness was destined to collapse rather suddenly about 50 miles later. But meantime, I saw my first Snowy Owl – looking, for all the world, like a giant seagull sawn off at the shoulders with a clown's face painted on the stump. It was a Harry Potter moment; it was magical.

The next section of track across to 'HMS Mercury' was enlivened by a diesel-tank oil-leak from a nearby barn, spilling along the dirt road in a thin trickle for an improbable distance. Had I been a smoker, the temptation to drop a match would have been irresistible; to look over my shoulder from the security of the next rise, as the livestock 'bought the farm' in a glorious fireball of succulent roast beef. The once-menacing 'HMS Mercury' was a 'stone frigate' commissioned during WW2. It used to sit ominously on Salt Hill like Noah's Ark; now only the straggly perimeter of barbed wire and security fencing remains.

Next up on the trail notes was Butser Hill, which gains its fearsome reputation from the challenging ascent climbing the reverse direction. Going east, it's just a steep grassy slope, like a newly mown lawn, dropping 600 feet. It looks unlikely that anyone could get into trouble here, but appearances can be deceptive. I'd argue that I'm optimistic rather than complacent. I'd chosen a dry day to be here, since wet grass, not to mention wet chalk, is lethal, especially riding on semi-slick tyres. But of

course, you don't need rain for grass to be wet at 8.00 am when the dew has yet to burn off.

I dropped in; whoosh; then I had second thoughts. I gently squeezed the brake levers passing 20 mph – to immediately lock both wheels and accelerate or seem to. It took an inordinately long time before my early-morning brain slipped into gear. I gently pulsed the levers and ever so slowly regained a measure of control. It was almost all over before it began.

The SDW then sweeps past the gentle contours of Grandfather's Bottom and ducks under the A3 main road before diving into the Queen Elizabeth Country Park. This is a popular mountain-bike playground, riven with a maze of steep downhill competition routes. As I got hopelessly lost here on last week's reccé, I stuck to the main drag and bid good-morning to the insomniac joggers and dog-walkers, exiting the park by the appositely named Head Down.

Kilometres of smooth riding on gravel trails and hard-pack country lanes followed, before crossing Harting Down. I passed a couple of young guys pushing their bikes up a small hill. This reinforced my entirely deluded impression of the task ahead and my capacity to complete it.

There are innumerable 'beacon hills' in England and there is another one on Harting Down. Untypically, the SDW approaches this killer slope on a well-graded diagonal so you can enjoy the scenery. But it's important to remember that every zig has its zag; the trail doubles back on itself and I missed the inflection.

Unplanned detour number one took me 2 miles out of my way, perhaps to atone for the mile and a half shaved off at the beginning of the ride. Ok fine, now we are even, but I could have done without detour number two, 15 miles later, which involved another five miles of diversion and 400 feet of extra climbing.

Detours are always downhill; it's hard to read a lichen-encrusted fingerpost at 20mph. The SDW is generally well signposted; however, some districts have done a better job than others. The problem is that you have to read the 'small print' or find that little acorn logo to distinguish a SDW sign from a regular bridleway. More confusing still, is that the SDW is also a part of the overall bridleway network, and sometimes that's all it says it is.

As an early user of GPS, my Garmin doesn't have preloaded maps; these only appear on the laptop when you download the ride data after you get home – always fun and often surprising. I had twenty A4 sheets of Ordinance Survey mapping in my backpack as a backup. But then, as each sheet only covered 5 miles, and I traversed the segments so quickly, I usually consulted the wrong map.

Back on track, head down, I crossed the Devil's Jumps – five Bronze Age bell-barrows – without really noticing them. In 1940, during the Battle of Britain, Hauptmann Oestermann crash-landed his Junkers 88 'Schnellbomber' aeroplane on this saw-tooth shrine to Beelzebub.

From here, the SDW passes through Lynchball Wood and Cocking Down. You cannot but love these English place names. Here, there are a number of chalk balls, each the size of a Smartcar, seemingly ditched by the trail-side. They are sculptures by Andy Goldsworth, but whether they honour the bravery of the WW2 flight crews or mock the cohunes of the lone SDW pilgrim, remains an open question.

I sprinted across the busy A286 and began the long, steep climb up into the Charlton Forest on Graffham Down. This climb was special; the landowner has recently surfaced the steepest section with billiard-table-smooth concrete. A guilty pleasure: but it won't last, homemade concrete roads never do.

I shot through Charlton Forest like Robin Hood on a mission, but then a bloody sheep passed me. I couldn't allow that. Granted, it was a fit-looking animal, but the honour of the 'Fat Tired Fabulists' was at stake. There was just enough field boundary to claim a dead heat.

The next section to Glatting Beacon involves another death-defying sprint across a main road – in this case the A285, and up another chalk hill. But surprisingly, overall, main roads are not a problem when traversing the SDW. In spite of its length, extending through half of South-east England, the route is crossed by just half-a-dozen main roads. The dual carriageways are bridged, but sometimes you have to wait a bit to cross a busy trunk road safely.

For most of the South Downs Way the trail ahead is in view as a thin white scar on the prospect slopes of an otherwise verdant landscape. Chalk, of course, is as white as white gets – something I should have considered when choosing glasses for the ride, especially when the sun came out later in the day.

Temporary snow-blindness, or its chalky equivalent, confuses depth perception and makes compliant front suspension more-or-less essential if one is to avoid headers. Another characteristic of 'the view in prospect' is that whenever you see a transmission tower on a distant hilltop, it's certain that you will include that punishing hilltop in your impending itinerary.

Next up was Bignor Hill, with the trail skirting yet another Neolithic camp, leaving the mysteries of Great Bottom and The Denture well to the south. The SDW stays on open grassland, before blowing all the height newly gained to cross the A23 and bridge the River Arun just north of Amberly.

I'd arranged to meet Alison outside the small town of Washington at Mile 56 on the SDW. I was riding substantially

229

unsupported, but my 'ride home' also carried bits and pieces, spare tyres, additional treats and flasks of hot coffee. More importantly, the little white Mini offered a friendly face and a little encouragement.

Alison phoned to say that she couldn't find the rendezvous point. At that moment, I was attempting to climb Amberley Mount, the first of the really hard slick-chalk ascents. It was hopeless, and I had to get off and push. Even then, I couldn't walk and talk at the same time, so I hung up.

The James Bond film 'A View to a Kill' was filmed here and perhaps the locals still gaze across the valleys with anticipation. The following 6 miles across Rackman Hill and the ancient Megalithic settlement of Rackham Banks seemed to take forever, but then it was a long swoop downhill to our rendezvous point at a car park off the A24.

For the first 50 miles of the SDW, I climbed every hill in the saddle, ate and drank on the go, agonised over the delay when filling water bottles and averaged about 10 miles per hour. The hours and miles clicked over precisely with sweet synchronicity.

I struggled for a few slow and painful miles, which included the 'lunch-stop'. Alison wasn't sure I should go on and I wasn't very sure either. It seems that I looked grey, tired and old. I couldn't eat, a bad sign, but the coffee was a welcome boost. In a moment of insight, I ditched my Camelback bladder of nauseating, pharmaceutically enhanced water, and took onboard a couple of bottles of very dilute lemon-squash.

Half an hour later, I got my second wind and wobbled off to climb Frieslands. But now I pushed up the heavy sections, stopped frequently to refuel, slowed to walking-pace to chat with each-and-every hiker, and struggled to average 8 miles an hour.

In the biting northerly, my optimistic 10-hour target-time blew through its window of chance and bowled off across the

English Channel. I had to accept that I wasn't half my age, and just completing the SWD would be an achievement. This new sustainability mode was perhaps realistic, but it was a major disappointment; it was crushing.

The SDW skirts Chantonbury Ring, an Iron Age hill fort also used by the Romans as a site for temples dedicated to a boar cult – to which this account may pay homage. It's a pretty spot; the defensive ramparts and dew pits are still visible. Hilltop living may be strategically sound, but it comes at a price – there is no running water. Consequently, there are dew pits throughout the South of England. Today they continue to serve the community as mountain-bike berms.

Following a couple of fairly relaxed miles on fast high-level grassland, the SDW skirts south of the Steyning Bowl and drops to sea-level again to pass through the small village of Botolphs and across the River Adur. One might expect the trail to take in a series of quintessentially English villages over the course of 100 miles but, surprisingly, it doesn't. There is just Easton, Botolphs, Alfriston and Jevington, all of which you are through before you know it, and that's it.

I nearly missed Botolphs altogether. My second unintended diversion took me on a swooping high-speed descent down a well-compacted, confidence inspiring gravel farm track, past the SDW turn-off and into Canada Bottom. I did suspect that I might be wrong this time, but it was such a great trail and the signposts looked fine, even if I passed too quickly to read them.

I was visually arrested however by the incongruous sight of a young, unaccompanied woman, in full black-on-black burqa gear, striding up the hill towards me, like the avenging wraith of age-inappropriate Lycra. I said hello and in return received a cheery greeting and, through the terrifying ocular slot, glimpsed an unexpected twinkle of the eye.

With that brief clash of cultures, the fun was over, and I had to forage back uphill to look for the real SDW. It had remained at altitude through this section to traverse a vast pig farm. I wound my way through mountainous heaps of pig-shit, piled high like a 'Dolomites in Miniature' porcine theme park. "*Do not feed the pigs*" said the signs. To be honest, it hadn't crossed my mind.

From Botolphs, I climbed the ancient, terraced slopes of Bleeding Hill and continued past Bushy Bottom, then on, to grind slowly up the innocent slopes of Truleigh Hill and Edburton Hill, skirting the ubiquitous prehistoric tumuli (barrows or hügelgräber). Close after Perching Hill, comes the splendidly named Fulking Hill, or perhaps another Fulking Hill.

There are too many myths and legends surrounding the dramatic landforms of the Devil's Dyke to recount here. The dyke was a magnet for Victorian day-trippers, but today is simply one of the best paragliding sites in the region. Alarmingly, it also appears to be an air traffic-free zone. As even the most minor collision would be fatal, the dashing flyers must have absolute faith in each other's ability.

The grass descent into Saddlescomb Dip was fast and easy, with the following section past Pyecomb and over the A273 tunnel also being cool-running on dry chalk. A long slog across Heathy Brow towards the Ditching Beacon followed, passing the picturesque, pre-carbon-fibre Jack and Jill windmills. The SDW crosses the Plumpton Plain (which it isn't) before heading south by Buckland Bank to bridge the A27, where poor Alison had been sitting in a lay-by for some time now, at SDW milepost 77.

The last few miles into our rendezvous at Housedean Farm were in complete contrast to the open grassland of Buckland. The trail is wooded, narrow and 'technical' in the

lethal sense. The badger community has toiled mightily to excavate huge holes every couple of metres through the fastest sections. I made it across but there were a few heart-in-mouth moments.

Whether disappearing down a badger burrow results in a Lewis Carrol-esque opium trip or a broken neck I do not know and, fortunately, was not driven to find out.

I released Alison from the cacophonous purgatory of the highway after couple of shots of caffeine and wee peck on the cheek and continued south on the single-track. The ascent from Loose Bottom to Swanborough Hill is a long slog, but not terribly difficult. But then, all of a sudden, I was subject to a vicious and apparently pre-meditated, attack on my person.

Half-way up, I was joined by a cock pheasant. This magnificent chap paced me while I chatted desultorily, making weak excuses for my slow rate of progress. I thought there was some empathy; I thought we had some sort of an understanding. I was therefore taken completely by surprise when the wee bugger went for my leg. I yelped and kicked him square in the chops.

Weary legs were now provoked into a little more action; yard-by-yard I opened out a safe distance. But my new friend 'Venal the Velociraptor' shadowed me until the gradient reversed in my favour through the prophetic Breaky Bottom. As I'd busted my ass for 83 miles at this point, I didn't need reminding in a placename.

I crossed the sludgy River Ouse and arrived at Southese Railway Station. God knows how this place survived the deprecations of Dr Beeching. It's in the middle of nowhere. But somehow, I see that the annual passenger numbers have doubled during the last decade. It's almost certain that the statistician responsible for these figures lives nearby and works in London.

There is a level-crossing with self-operation for authorised key-holders. I am not an 'authorised key-holder'. The gates were locked and there was no green light. I had no idea if a train was coming or not, so to play safe I slipped into the deserted station and carried my bike over the footbridge.

Running parallel to the railway is the A26, with a rather easier crossing via a brand-new cycle bridge; but I guess the slats have been nailed on from the bottom-up as I immediately got a puncture. Never mind; the sun had come out, so I carried the Merlin up to the top of Ilford Hill, sat down, munched a Mars Bar and set to work.

I'm not religious but I am worryingly superstitious. I believe that the more spare tubes you carry, the less likelihood there is of a puncture. Kevlar linings, reinforced sidewalls, Slime – these things make no difference whatsoever in my experience. I carried 3 spare tubes and a puncture repair outfit, so my luck held out to SDW mile-85. One more tube and I'd have made it to Eastbourne.

There is no point in changing the tube unless you can find out what caused the puncture, otherwise it's easy to quickly run through your total supply of spares; but could I find the cause? Eventually, after a long and fruitless search I fitted another tube and pumped it up. It was still up when I wrote this.

I cycled nervously past Red Lion Pond and White Lion Pond, home to the Silver Spotted Skipper or Hesperia Comma butterfly. Fifteen miles to go; I thought I was almost there. Field followed tussocky field and soon I began to long for hard-pack trails to translate my efforts into forward motion.

Grass is fun at first, but it does get tiring; same goes for herding sheep and slaloming sheep shit. But at least sheep don't block the gates and face you down with a truculent stare. The beasts on guard here are cattle. Bullocks seem bigger now than when I was a boy; and, thanks to steroids, I expect they are.

Only later, did I stumble across some research on the difference between riding across meadows and hard-pack surfaces. See Chapter No.76 'Rolling Stock-taking'.

Where were we? Males Burgh, Firle Beacon, Bostal Hill and then down into the pretty village of Alfriston, just seven and a half miles from my destination at Eastbourne Pier. I chatted to an old couple who teased me that it was only another 30 miles to go. And weirdly, by some quirk of Einstein's Theory of Special Relativity, as applied to sexagenarian mountain-bikers, space and time did indeed spread out by a factor of four.

The final run over to Eastbourne is via an incredibly steep hill. Had I looked at the profile, that much would have been obvious. Moreover, these historic bridleways are rocky and eroded, flaunting the pillage residue of ancient Roman cobbles.

At Windover Hill, the famous 'Long Man of Wilmington' is revealed in chalk, 235 feet high on the north face; I went right past it. On finally through Jevington, home of the now world-famous Banoffee Pie and up again along the longest 2 miles in England and into Eastbourne. My dusty tyres kissed the urban asphalt with blessed relief. I whooped and swooped into the city, covering the last 3 miles in 12 minutes on residual adrenaline.

Alison was waiting to greet me at Eastbourne Pier, with her smiley-faced wee Mini Clubman parked nearby to augment the welcoming party of one. Total ride time in the saddle was 11.30 including about half an hour of detours, with maybe another hour for lunch, punctures and afternoon tea. Total distance on the Garmin GPS was 106 miles with over 13,000 feet of climbing. Average Heart Rate 130. Total number of flies swallowed: 3.

The approach to Salt Hill, SDW, Hampshire. Image - the Author

236

Tar bubbles

2013, Hampshire: The unmistakable sound of depilatory tape interrupts my concentration as I blitz through the Civil War battle ground of Cheriton, head down, in the drops, on the road-bike. No, I haven't slipped over the edge, daydreaming about becoming as 'mamils' do with their shiny legs, replica team kit and associated pro-cyclist delusions.

The idiotic top-dressing, smeared everywhere across the road pavement this spring by Hampshire County maintenance crews, has melted. I am grinding through gooey tarmac which adheres to my tyres like Velcro. The road and rubber separate with that distinctive sticky rasp that recalls the one and only time I accompanied Alison to a beauty clinic and waited outside while she had a leg wax.

It's been a hot summer. It's been hot like it used to be hot when we were shirtless kids in shorts and sandals, sporting cowboy neckerchiefs. I lived in Equatorial Asia for 30 years and didn't see very much melted asphalt. Maybe the composition is different there, like the unmeltable bars of milk chocolate.

Ready-to-lay asphalt occurs naturally on a small island in Sulawesi. Buton's economy is based around the export of asphalt to Japan. Four hundred million tons of the stuff lies in reserve. The deposit is not a big black lake, as in Trinidad, but already bound up in a 20/80 aggregate, which you can more-or-less roll straight onto the road, without any meddling by the likes of John McAdam.

As an interesting aside, ignoring for the moment their admittedly amoral predilection for piracy and slave-trading, during the 14th century, Buton's Wolio-Hindu community developed an effective proto-democratic society. In order to preserve the principles of a democratic monarchy, the sovereign's rights of patronage were tightly reigned in.

Unusually for a fairy-tale kingdom, there were no dashing princes nor, alas, languid princesses provocatively dangling braided pigtails from the battlements of the Kraton palace. Reigning kings were not allowed to sew the royal seed, on pain of death, as this might produce a prince or princess with a claim to the throne. And with no hereditary dimensions, there was none of that inbreeding that blights European royal families.

When Samuel was a wee boy his favourite thing was scootering back and forth across bubble-wrap. The trrrrrrr-aaaaaaaa-ppppppp of bursting bubbles is intoxicating. We've had that here too; zipping over the glistening tar bubbles on the back roads surely heralds a second childhood.

Samuel above Loch Goil, Argyll, Scotland. Go-Pro image – the Author

Idjoch, Austria/Switzerland. Image - Aberdeen Banker

239

The Coffin Train, Switzerland. Image - Wolfgang Burghofer

Reading between the lines

2013, Austria, Switzerland and Italy: This year finally saw the full team assembled in Axams to ride Ulli Stanciu's Route No.5, 'Tracciolino', a ride named after an extraordinary final day in the mountains above Lake Como. The tour rates a maximum 5 out of 5 for 'climbing', 'distance', 'altitude', 'value of experience' and 'required physical condition'. So, it was obvious this wasn't going to be a push-over.

Still, there was a little less serious climbing indicated vis-a-vis previous tours, the challenge appeared modulated to match our diminishing super-powers, and the complete package seemed feasible for the fragile sexagenarian in our midst. Yea right.

I arrived in Innsbruck a few days early. Fritz picked me up from the airport and we collected a brand-new 'Specialized Stumpjumper FSR Comp' from i-bikes. Then we settled in to embark on the first of the series of 'welcome', 'depart', 'return' and 'farewell' parties that inevitably bracket visits to the home of Fritz and Erika.

As luck would have it, we all arrived in Axams at different times so the parties count soared and the schnapps toasts multiplied accordingly. Fritz regards all this as 'training' – if you can handle the parties, he reckons the ride is a foregone conclusion. Fritz, however, doesn't have a hiatus hernia.

I took the big 29er up the Lizum behind Axams the next morning. I'd never ridden a big wheel mountain bike. I was unconvinced about the marketing claims but was of an open

mind at this stage. Fritz joined me for another ride in the afternoon. We ascended the Nockhofweg, behind Mutters – that ran the total metres of climbing for the day up to 1,500, burned a few calories and worked up a modest thirst, the last of which was particularly useful.

Steffen arrived that night, after a long day-long drive across Europe, from Denmark through Germany, so we planned some more acclimatisation for the next day, to give the lowlanders an even chance against the gradient-hardened Austrian mountain men. I suggested climbing the Senderstal, the next valley to the west of Axams, and we embarked on this the following morning.

Unfortunately, my intended route was not in fact the next valley, which lacks a café, but the next but one. We topped-out the Senderstal, descended rapidly and started all over again up the Fotschertal. As these two valleys are the scenic-equal of anything thrown up in a Trans-Alps, this wasn't a problem, and it gave us another 2,000-metre ascent to stretch our legs for the main event.

Steffen was better equipped and better prepared than ever. He had been training at sea-level in the damp, grey, murder capital of Europe for five-long-years. In fact, as the day wore on, it became clear that the understated Great Dane was ominously fit. I began to think I should have invested in more training after the 'South Downs Way' back in May, rather than propped in the catenary repose of a Dali-esque melt down, resting on my laurels.

Wolfgang arrived next morning, chaperoned by Erika, who had travelled to Upper Austria to rescue him from the excesses of a long evening carousing with a local male-voice-choir. We slung the four bikes on the roof of Fritz's Supersportwagen and set off for St Anton. Karen, Fritz's Office

Manager, came along to take the car back. Later, back in Innsbruck, Fritz commented on the impressive number of dead insects splattered on the Audi's grill. Karen clearly doesn't hang about when she gets behind the wheel.

Day 1: We saddled up in a car park in downtown St. Anton, an expensive resort where the British and Swedish royal families enjoy the peerless gravity of the Austrian ski slopes. From here, we swiftly left the secondary road network behind to follow a well-graded gravel road to the Konstanzer Huette at 1,866 metres. This was the first of many strudel and Coke stops. Indeed, this particular tour is so well serviced by mountain huts, ski stations, roadside cafes and hotels that we lugged several kilos of meticulously planned energy supplements to Italy and then all the way back, with scarcely a dent in the stash.

The gravel road eventually folded into an interesting single-track as far as a little wooden bridge where it ramped up abruptly. I once heard a particularly steep road described as 'a plank laid against the sky'; this trail fitted that description.

We pushed and occasionally dragged our bikes up to the Kleine Scheidseen, a plateau peppered with hill-top tarns. The trail was again rideable, but a lot of snow remained to make life difficult. I tried to cross the residual drifts every-which-way, but without conspicuous success. We slithered and tumbled across a long mile of snowfields all the way to the Heilbronner Huitte at 2,320 metres.

This hut has become a popular stop-over on Trans-Alps, overnight tours and day trips. Fredi Immler, the manager of the hut, regards the new generation of extreme bikers as "*a gift from God*"; and certainly, the hungry downhill guys must be welcome business through the summer months. A youthful contingent of roly-poly 'long-travel' bikers was leaving as we arrived.

It's interesting that, although we were on a well-known long-distance route, during the short weather window when these trips are possible, we did not meet anyone else on an extended tour. My guess is that most guys you meet on the hill have been teleported there via the cable-car network, content with just the 'downside' of great mountain biking.

Apfelstrudel and coffee this time, with the observation that the strudel was becoming fatter and yet more delicious as we travelled south. The afternoon rain was on the way, so we paid our bill and dropped into the fast downhill to the Zeinisjoch. However, as often on fast and furious descents, we arrived at the bottom of the hill to find ourselves somewhere unexpected.

As a result, we enjoyed an unplanned early excursion out of Tyrol and into Vorarlberg. Somewhere along the way we rolled along the European watershed. To the west the rivulets flow to the Rhine and the North Sea, to the east they trickle off to the Danube and the Black Sea.

Eventually, we found the minor road to Galtür that we were looking for. Back in 1999, there was a disastrous avalanche here which killed 31 people. Relatively warm weather in January of that year was directly followed by record snowfalls and strong February winds. This led to the build-up of an exceptionally large and unstable accumulation on the slopes above Galtür. A 170,000-tonne block of snow broke away near the top of the mountain and accelerated to 300 kph. It took less than a minute to hit Galtür on the valley floor.

Help arrived, and traumatised tourists were evacuated, via an air-bridge using NATO Black Hawk choppers. The tragedy accelerated the pace of research into avalanches and transformed their management. It also prompted a crazy, but ultimately vital experiment with a manned bunker located directly in the path of the avalanche chute at Vallée de la Sionne.

Today, there are a dozen extremely substantial protection and diversion structures, constructed after the fashion of the Inca's massive stonework at Machu Picchu. None of this can have been economically viable, nor can it have been easy to retain faith in the security of the community. But, in the face of such adversity, Galtür has endured.

The morning road-transfer had limited our riding time on this first day. We had cycled 50 tough kilometres and climbed 1,500 metres during the afternoon, so we elected to knock off early and check in overnight in Ischgl. This is another up-market resort noted for the high-life, dancing on the table and generally excessive après-ski.

After the usual riding about, just as the torrential afternoon rains arrived, we decided on the Hotel Ferienglück, a reasonably-priced four-star lodge. We cleaned up and assembled in the bar to plan Day 2 and the next stage. Steffen took a beautifully lit photo of this, which evokes the conspirators of the Gunpowder Plot.

Day 2: Next morning, we found ourselves dithering about in the foothills, looking for the best way up. The climb is unrelenting: 12.5 kilometres ascending 1,500 metres to the Idjoch. Consequently, our gung-ho guru, hard-man Uli, unusually recommends the cable car – "*massively steep*" he says, with a 20% gradient.

But the Fat-tired Fabulists are not fabulists for nothing; so, we resolved to cycle, despite having a free pass on the cable-car as part of our hotel package! Our navigation brains-trust elected for a direct assault via a crooked dirt road by a gully at the back of town – a route requiring us to thread through precariously poised earth-moving equipment.

The engineer in charge of works advised us to double-back; but, fortunately, I don't speak German and Fritz is also

an engineer – so he tendered a contrary second opinion. In any case, the road was not exactly 'closed' closed; we just had to phone ahead from time to time for permission to bypass, variously: forest operations; landslip reconstruction; and rockfalls. It all went swimmingly; apart from an attempt by a timber truck, laden with unsnedded timber, to sideswipe us off a tight hairpin with a giant broom of Norwegian Spruce.

A pattern for the week was established. Fritz and I formed a sensibly paced peloton and the other two indulged in long, lung-burning breakaways. I had stolen a jump on Steffen to take the 'Spotted Jersey' at the Heilbronner Huitte the day before – by riding him into a handily-placed mini-busload of dozy tourists. But it was now clear that that moment of glory was unlikely to be repeated.

After an interminable but not in fact impossible grind, morning coffee at the Idalpe Ski Station was more than welcome. This is a beautiful, five-star facility where aging rock stars consort with celebrities of doubtful worth; consequently, the manager warmly received four bandanaed bikers and treated us royally.

The apfelstrudel alone was worth the climb, not to mention the pure pleasure of squiggling saddle-sore bums into the sheepskin throws on the director's chairs.

From here we had a shorter but still demanding uphill section to the Idjoch. A gravel service road runs from the cable car station skywards to the Greitspitze. On the way up, we met a friendly ex-banker from Aberdeen who recognised my in-your-face **Scotland** cycling jersey, unnoticed so far by my lexicologically challenged companions. We talked about student life in Castle Street in the 1970s and he took our photo. I must apologise here to my new friend's good lady wife, as I 'Photoshopped' her out of the final image.

We stopped at the Idjoch for a photo-call at the old Swiss border post. Switzerland is not a member of the EU, much less signatory to the 'Schengen Agreement' on open borders, but it pretends it is and has abandoned these remote ridgeline stations. Then we continued along the bald scree ridge to the Greitspitze.

The Greitspitze was the high point of our trip at 2,864 metres (prosaically, but sadly not existentially). As a peak, it's not exactly photogenic; it brings to mind a vast inside-out quarry. It's a desolate, God-forsaken spot. But it is a splendid platform from which to enjoy an incredible 360⁰ panorama of drop-dead gorgeous Alpine scenery.

The GPS route-finder was 'acting up' so we missed the Salaaser trailhead; or maybe we didn't, as the remnants of a ridgeline trail appeared from time to time on our right; but the description was somewhat at odds with the reality – remodelled through cable-car construction works-access. We definitely missed the valley section, which eventually appeared several hundred metres below us. In the end, we somehow descended to the Zeblasjoch at 2,539 metres, rather than climbing up to it as the route guide suggested.

No matter, we were now on the Zeblas Supertrail, constructed by Erwin Jehle specifically for mountain bikers some years ago. Uli has this to say: "*this trail rejoices the heart; if any trail is a trail that 'flows' then this is it: gliding at speed through Alpine meadows, the happy rider will yodel himself hoarse.*"

But Fritz had other ideas. We took a left turn and embarked on a direct ascent of the snow-capped 2,752-metre Fuorcia Val Gronda – well Steffen and I did. Meanwhile, the Brains Trust reviewed their decision and shortly thereafter we were recalled to follow the Zeblas. This was probably a good idea since Uli's 'Option B' for super-strong bikers involved at

least 500 vertical metres of desperate hands-and-feet climbing, all portage in deep snow.

The Zeblas was fine and actually is mostly 'bikeable', until it ended abruptly at an enormous hole in the ground. I was riding like hell with my head down concentrating furiously. Fortunately, there is a fence. As our friend Uli likes to advise us, 'rideability' is a relative term.

I was beginning to have misgivings about the 29er FSR. The main issue was that the beast is so much longer, and thus less agile, than a regular bike. A 29" wheel bike should logically be just 6" longer than a 26", but it's more like 9" due to the rear suspension configuration and the slack steering angle. On open ground or big downhills this isn't an issue, in fact it's an asset; but on tight single-track, the bike is about as agile as a tandem.

Back to the big hole: it was not a bike trap but dug to accommodate the foundations of a terminus for the new cable-car to the Fuorcia Val Gronda. As we approached the site works, we were impressed by a tightly orchestrated three-chopper relay, shuttling open hoppers of wet concrete from the road-end up to the summit of mountain. Such complex engineering operations are mesmerising.

We carried our bikes around the site perimeter and continued downhill on the gravel service road, dodging a hefty cement mixer wheezing its way up. After topping up with water at the Verbellabach River, we joined the tourist-track to the Heilbronner Huette at 2,320 metres, arriving in the middle of the forecast mid-afternoon downpour. As often, following Uli's gruelling detours, and our own maundering variations, we wondered why we hadn't just cycled up the road from Ischgl like everyone else.

The Heilbronner is a big, well-equipped mountain inn, so we took advantage of the opportunity to dry off and fill our

bellies with Inge Huber's excellent noodle soup, before embarking on the gruesome Fimberpass. My old mate Chris and his aging ski-buddies make an annual tour in the Alps. They have started three tours from here, so I knew it would be a special area. But no one told me it was an accursed 'coffin trail'.

The Paznaun Valley (where Galtür and Ischgl are sited) once belonged to the Municipality of Sent in Switzerland. As late as 1616, the grateful dead of this out-of-the-way community were brought across the Fimberpass to the graveyards of Sent. It was a gruelling 10-hour trudge for the pallbearers. In winter, when the track from Ischgl became impassable, the Swiss coffin-convoy simply stacked up the boxes in the perfect deep freeze of this high valley and waited until spring to transport the by-now-conveniently plank-like corpses over the pass.

After I wrote this rather flippant description, Alfred Hofer, a 60-year-old biker on a fully supported commercial tour, fell to his death on the Fimberpass descent. Dreadful news. No one signs up for that.

The route-description concedes that only short sections of the steep track leading up to the Fimberpass are 'bikeable', but we had a good crack at it and reached the top in under an hour. The view from the Fimberpass back to the Fluchthorn and ahead into the Engadin Mountains of Switzerland is awesome and certainly worth the struggle to get there. However, it was getting late, we were tired, and we had to press on to complete the day's assigned mileage.

Uli informs us that, "*the downhill trail to Zuort is extremely demanding.*" He notes further that: "*Readers of my previous book have complained that it is not bikeable.*" Nothing if not thorough, our sage went back to check it out: "*I have done it again and realised that some sections have been heavily washed-out, and riding has become more difficult. Nevertheless, 'bikeability' is a relative term. Forgetting*

about the washed-out sections, free-riders will enjoy this section, less skilled riders will have to push."

Unfortunately, despite Fritz translating this information with unerring accuracy, the crucial text lay folded and undisturbed in my backpack. And, as custodian of perhaps the most downhill-specific bike in the party, I had a misplaced sense of duty to play the role of 'miner's canary', or in this instance 'crash-test dummy'. I set the shocks to long-travel, lowered the saddle all the way down and clipped in.

I didn't get far.

Sometimes in the mountains, the lie of the landscape makes it difficult to judge the precise gradient of a slope. Sometimes, water seems to run uphill; and sometimes, steep is not just steep, it's slithery. These illusions are quickly dispelled when you are walking. However, mountain-bikers occupy what we might term a 'non-linear gravitational environment'.

I realised that I was in trouble right away. You might also remember that we had scuttled into to Inge Huber's hostelry to escape a heavy downpour earlier; so, realistically, I didn't stand a chance. I decided to bail out. Whether this was big mistake or a divinely inspired move, I'm still not sure. Wolfgang was behind me and saw what happened.

Zero adhesion and overwhelming gravity meant that a dignified dismount was impossible. I executed a couple of stylish forward rolls, with the bike attached to my feet through the first of these. I slithered inexorably to the edge of the trail, then over it, coming to rest on an outcrop of frost-shattered shale.

As the keeper of the first-aid kit, I was well into damage control when the rest of the team arrived. But there was still a long way to go before I could put my feet up. And, of course, this section of the route took longer that it might have had we not been cautious to a fault during the remainder of the descent.

I stumbled through the course of the long, late-afternoon, leaning heavily on the bike and compounding the damage to be dealt with later. Following watercourses along the path of least resistance, we missed the turn-off to Val Sinestra and ended up paralleling Uli's route on a similar track on the wrong side of the valley. But by this point we, or at least I, was past caring. We zipped through Vna and arrived, exhausted in Romosch, with a total ascent of 2,850 metres clocked on the GPS.

Alas, there was 'no room at the inn', so we continued for another 10km to Scuol, and checked into the plush 'Panorama', a small boutique hotel, sometime after 7.00 p.m. Our hostess made us welcome, but it was explained that we would have to go across the street for dinner, as she had recently given up the gastgeberin side of the business.

She told us that: "*When my guests are fast asleep in their rooms, they are no trouble; in the restaurant, with a few drinks inside them, it's another matter entirely.*" However, she did provide us all with matching snow-white slippers to facilitate our foraging excursion across the road. And the dear lady did produce an excellent breakfast next morning.

Fritz had negotiated a fair fixed price for our laundry, so we threw everything bar our bicycles into the basket and headed upstairs to seek resurrection beneath long hot showers and half an hour of sensory delight beneath crisp white linen. But then, as I peeled off my shredded, muddy Lycra, it became obvious that there might be a change of plans in prospect.

Bloody shins and other odd abrasions cleaned up well enough, but when I put on my glasses and looked beyond that, I couldn't ignore two ominously puffed-up and tender ankles and an enormous, painful, purple foot.

There goes another metatarsal, the third break on the same damn foot. It was depressing to say the least, or "*Sh!t, Sh!t, Sh!t,*

Sh!t, Sh!t", as I muttered at the time. I mummified both my poor wee feet in the remaining bandages from our first aid kit, swallowed a handful of painkillers and hobbled downstairs to join the party.

We all enjoyed an excellent dinner at the Hotel Bellaval and downed a few more beers than normal to celebrate out safe arrival at the tour's mid-point. In such cases of regret and self-recrimination, the demon drink has welcome palliative properties, it's mildly antiseptic and it's a peerless over-the-counter analgesic. I can thoroughly recommend it.

However, despite all this dedicated rehab, when bedtime came around, I discovered that I was stranded, virtually immobile in the restaurant. Young Wolfgang had to more-or-less carry me back across the road to our digs.

Day 3: *"But when the strong were too weak to hurt the weak, the weak had to be strong enough to leave."* So said Milan Kundera in 'The Unbearable Lightness of Being'. Whatever it means, it seemed apt that morning. However, at breakfast, before I could offer myself for self-sacrifice and emulate my boyhood hero, Captain Lawrence Oates, I was swiftly dumped. On occasions like this, a natural leader always steps forward. It was Fritz who broke the news gently by extolling the virtues of the Swiss Railways network.

There was some debate about where I would meet up with the lads – next overnight stop, or even back at Axams. The team eliminated Tiefencastel and then Bergun opportunities for a potential rendezvous, before deciding on Silvaplana. Despite assertions to the contrary, it was clear to me that, for the moment at least, the programme was being sublimated to keep the door open for me. In the revised route, they had effectively bypassed the super-tough hiking sections of the Fourcla da Funtauna and Septimer Pass.

Fritz outlined a relatively easy day, with just 1,500 metres of climbing along the margins of the fledgling Inn River, all well below the snowline. The 'story' was that extreme trails were ok; but there seemed little point in carrying your bike up a mountain when you also had to carry it down the other side. Ergo, why bother with the bike at all? I went along with the charade and went back to bed, to rest up until lunchtime.

Late morning, I got kitted up and prepared to check out. The first challenge was getting my shoes on; this was achieved by stages – with useful compression and support as a by-product. Then there was the question of making the damaged bike roadworthy, mainly straightening the warped rear brake disk one millimetre at a time with my bare hands. At this point, the whole enterprise was in the balance.

I hobbled across the road to the Scuol railhead and bought tickets for me and the bike to Samedan – 20SFr for one and 18SFr for the other. It's a superb rail-journey along the exquisite Engadine Valley. Steffen took a picture of my train as I clickety-clicked past the humble cyclists on my regal way through.

Freewheeling out of Samedan Station, I headed in the general direction of St Moritz. I didn't have a map, but there is an extensive, braided network of bike-trails through this region, catering for all levels of fitness and ability. I found that, despite some eye-watering limitations in relation to the twist-release on the SPD pedals, I could manage the 'Alpine' tagged trails and so avoid the indignity of 'mixing it' with e-bikes and family outings.

With a significant head-start on the boys, I could afford to dawdle. I stopped off for a coffee in St Moritz and then enjoyed an ice-cream at the kitesurfing centre in Silvaplana, before doubling back along the Champfer Lake. Eventually I ran out of things to do and climbed into the hills to find a nice spot for a snooze in the sunshine.

I kept in touch with Fritz on the phone and we met up outside town before checking into the faux-ramshackle Ferienhotel Julier Palace. We negotiated four rooms of widely differing standard for the same exorbitant price, but somehow everyone drew the short straw.

In the Alps, iced water is available on tap. I took advantage of that, while catching up with the day's events at the Tour de France. Dinner was distinguished by Fritz and I sharing our soup from the same bowl – shocking to our fellow diners and clearly not very Swiss.

Day 4: Next morning, a remotivated rolled out of town all-together, with various route options on the table. We planned to salvage our tour by re-joining Uli's programme and doubling the famous Tracciolino railroad. It was mostly downhill. My GPS recorded about 2,350 metres descent through the day, with just 700 metres of climbing over the course of 75 kilometres, as the temperature rose inexorably from 9^0C to 35^0C.

There were sections of forest road and some rocky single-track but, most of the way, we followed asphalt or designated cinder bike-trails. I was quite happy about this, as the 'more interesting' bumpy sections of the descent turned my ride into an exercise in 'algiatry through psychokinesis', or pain management through mind over matter.

Our route diversion wasn't extreme in relation to the physical challenge, but the scenery was to die for. Up above the mirror-like Lake Sils, snapping frame after frame, we seemed to have lost the thread of hard-core biking and metamorphosed into Japanese shutterbugs. We stopped for morning coffee at Maloja, then launched over the pass at 1,815 metres, which plummets to Casaccia on the floor of the Orlegna Valley in just a few kilometres. At this point, we were back on Uli's tried and tested tour route.

From Casaccia we diverted again to explore some promising gravel trails and rocky single-track past Vicosoprano and Stampa, paralleling the Via Principale to Soglio on the Italian border. On the way, we stopped to admire the mighty Albigna Dam, sited high on the southern wall of the valley. Very few massive, man-made structures co-exist tolerably well with outstanding natural landscapes, but this is one of them. Fritz inevitably slipped into power-station tour-guide mode.

From time to time, we were obliged to use the main road. I struggled to keep up with the others as we swooped at breakneck speed beneath claustrophobic landslip canopies and through mesmerising, stroboscopic tunnels.

Our little peloton shot through the gaping border post like startled rumrunners and promptly nipped into Soglio for lunch. Italy, fantastic! Switzerland is great but chaotic, cheap-and-cheerful Italy is even better. We ordered huge quantities of pasta and pizza and basked in the sunshine. Our new plan was to carry on to Verceia, spend the night there and then hit the Trancciolio early before the day-trippers arrived.

We closed-up to form an aerodynamic road train and hammered the almost-deserted bikeways. The only event of note was a long time-out under the high-tension powerlines in Chiavenna. The GPS roadbook encouraged us to go first one way, then the other.

Many GPS-equipped surveyors have experienced signal degradation in such locations, so tracker confusion is always possible. It's the pylons rather than the wires that cause the problem, apparently, although in our case it was heat exhaustion! Steffen and I hunkered down in the shade as the temperatures soared into the high thirties.

Eventually, we reached Verceia, a small town in the throes of picturesque decay. The commune occupies a small delta

projecting into Lake Mezzola, formed from the terminal moraine of the wonderfully named 'Torrenti Ratti'. As it transpired, at dusk that evening a sudden, violent downpour would wash away several sections of the Rats Valley road which gives access to the Tracciolino: rats!

The beach hotel in Verceia has closed down, so we backtracked to Novate Mezzola looking for a place to stay. We sat down on a sidewalk in the old town, while Fritz organised bed and breakfast with, of all people, the local land surveyor (but, disappointingly, failed to resolve the powerline, GPS debate).

As we waited for out host to turn up, we were ambushed by an entrepreneurial ice-cream vendor....and surrendered happily. The hotelier arrived and led us by car (wing mirrors folded) through the narrow, cobbled streets to meet his wife and check in.

Rather than shower, we grabbed towels and cycled down to the lake for a swim. This seemed a good idea at the time but, if you are familiar with the construction of cycling shorts, the downside was sundowners sat on soggy sponge.

We took a table in the Beach Bar beside an old Windglider sailboard (as used in the 1984 Los Angeles Olympics) erected like a giant tombstone in the sand. Thousands of these horrible sailboards have found new life in this capacity, blazoning beach bars throughout the world. Fred Ostermann, the designer, must be proud.

There aren't many restaurants in Novate, so we returned to our digs by way of the supermarket, where we picked up a portable-feast of bread, ham and cheese; and in a nostalgic tribute to our generation's first encounter with wine in the 1970s, 2 litres of Chianti in a fat, raffia-wrapped bottle.

I was immensely encouraged when Fritz fell off his bike in the carpark and the evening just got better after that. Well, up

until the moment when our landlady popped her head in, with a gentle request to moderate our mirth. It seems the 'old dragon next door' was ever on the look-out for some transgression of the commune ordinance, and raucous, self-catering dinner-parties are "*not normale*" in the B&B business.

Next morning, we were all up surprisingly bright and early. I was in mind-over-matter mode and we were ready to go. Uli reckons that, "*you will not find a more spectacular and exciting finish of a Transalp*" and as it transpired, none of us would disagree. Today was the day.

When you arrive in Verceia, there is no obvious way up. The access zigzags up the gullet of the chundering Torrenti Ratti for a steep climb of 1,000 vertical metres on the grandly named 'Via XXV Aprile' – when Italy was liberated from the Italians!

The builder of a little house under construction on a non-existent site between two hairpins called out "*Tracciolino?*" "*Yes*" we replied. "*Buono, baldo, baldo!*" That's what you get when you wear red bandanas! Then we met a disgruntled cyclist bounced at the road works and coming back down much earlier in the day than he expected. But when you travel with an engineering consultant in attendance, no road is closed; so, we bypassed the taciturn roadbuilders and continued on up.

The Tracciolino 'trail' follows a narrow-gauge railway built in the 1930s as part of a modest hydro project which taps the Torrenti Ratti. The famous trail is cut into the vertical rock wall of the massif and being a railway, is entirely flat. The railway section is extended by an inspection track carved out in the same fashion, though rather narrower and more precarious.

There are substantially intact guard-wires strung along the length of the railway, but these become increasingly unreliable, then intermittent before eventually disappearing in the less-accessible reaches of the footway.

We scrambled up the last few metres to the rail track past a mysterious excavation at the road-end. The path was steep and narrow and carpeted with loose rubble; even so, the workmen 10 metres below us had no hard hats and no concerns.

Wolfgang lifted my bike round the barrier and gave me a hand up and suddenly we were there. I couldn't quite believe it. We clowned around, as you would expect, and took some photos of ourselves posing beside the smart new 'Private Property, No Access, No Cycling, Danger of Landslides' sign.

We went right first and explored the Valley of the 'Rats River'. The railway terminates at a small high dam, with Fritz was once more in his element explaining the clever features of the spillway design. Meanwhile, Wolfgang, who shares the Felix Baumgartner gene, posed on precipitous ledges, before assuming photographic duties for the rest of the afternoon.

The sleepers are well-ballasted so it's not difficult to cycle across them, between the lines. The rattle-and-bump rhythm is actually quite reassuring. Well, that is unless there is a train coming the other way. We all thought this was marvellous, but we had seen nothing yet; we had yet to discover genuine 'mountain-biking sex'.

After a couple of kilometres, we passed the celebrated 'long tunnel' which branches off to the right and continued to the wagon-lift which once raised fully laden rail wagons all the way from Verceia up onto the Tracciolino. Sadly, today, all this marvellous Heath Robinson engineering is obsolete, rusting and abandoned.

We doubled back to the tunnel entrance and fished out our mini-bike-lights for comparison, all powered by the same little lithium button-cell batteries. Fritz's were great, Steffen's good, Wolfgang's barely adequate and mine worse-than-useless. Inside the entrance, there is a little metal box and inside that is

a secret switch; alas, each filament in the passageway merely sheds light on a saucer-sized smudge of tunnel roof.

Riding the tunnel without a powerful headlamp becomes an exercise in joining the dots while staying between the (invisible) lines. 700mm is a lot narrower in the dark than it is in daylight. Never mind, there is light at the end of the tunnel, even if it is 400 metres away. It's dank and slippery and smells like a crypt; it's just magic.

At the end of the long tunnel, the railway lines disappear into another tunnel; this one is closed and locked. But that isn't a problem; the inspection track continues, as if carved across the rock face by a giant router. It's hard to imagine a more spectacular trail: exposed ledges, dizzy overhangs, frequent tunnels, vertical drops and always spectacular views across Lake Mezzla, Como and the southern Italian Alps.

If not for the surviving old guard-wires in the most exposed sections, it would be almost impossible to cycle here. I say 'almost' only because I have seen my Austrian friends defy vertigo, logic, and good old-fashioned common sense when given half a chance, so I assume that they can also defy gravity.

The narrow half-tunnel cuts horizontally across the landscape for kilometre after kilometre towards the Codera Valley. Initially it's hard to believe that you can ride the Tracciolino without being arrested or coming to grief, and then it's hard to believe that a trail of this quality can go on and on.

With growing confidence, we quickly learned to manage our momentum and ride securely. When you are rolling, faster is safer. Speed smoothed our passage through the rock-gardens and the magic of centripetal force glued us to the trail on tight concave bends where gully erosion had invariably washed-out the apex.

Ten kilometres in, the trail became overgrown and less defined. There were more and more rockfalls and the guard-

wires disappeared altogether. It looked like the end of the line. Fritz picked up his bike and disappeared into the bush; he didn't return, so we followed. The magic trail reappeared through a wooded section, but here it was completely undisturbed – clearly no one had been through here on a bike this season.

Eventually, we came across the tunnel collapse that now effectively ends the ride within sight of Codera. The community of Codera is the last village in Europe without vehicular access; a return trip to the shops involves 5,000 steps and, doubtless, a damn-fit donkey.

The return trip is not an anti-climax. It provides a completely different perspective on the marvellous scenery and another 10km of a unique cycling experience. None of us will forget our adventure on the Tracciolino. It is, without question, the most fun anyone could ever have on a mountain-bike.

Rolling back down the '25th of April highway' dodging dozy day-trippers on the way up, I could now weigh our setbacks against what we had gained, and for the first time in three days I reckoned we were in credit. It was finally worth all the discomfort; and remained so, despite the long-drawn-out recovery period.

The 'Fat-tired Fabulists' lingered over a late lunch of pasta before the leisurely ride down to Colico on Lake Como where we treated ourselves handsomely to rooms on the front at the Hotel Risi, rendezvoused with Fritz's friend Wolfgang who was to ferry our trick-cycling-circus back to Austria and generally rounded out the trip in the usual excessive style.

Well, that is, until the big party back in Axams.

So, it wasn't a Trans-Alps that pushed the boundaries in relation to endurance, speed or daring; I climbed just 10,000 metres, as opposed to 14,500 the last time. For me at least, the tour was all about pain; and any achievement was in relation to

handling it. But to be honest, had there been a voiture balai in attendance I'd have been in it like a shot.

"For a cyclist, pain is a familiar - and valuable - companion. I would not exactly call pain a friend. But it is a constant companion in my life. Sometimes I say that pain is my favourite enemy. We have this love-hate relationship. We keep watching each other and waiting for the other one to show some weakness, to give in. Every morning when I jump on my bike, it takes only seconds for me to think, 'Ah, there you are my old enemy; let's get it on for one more day!' The pain and me, nothing can keep us apart. It keeps me going. It keeps me young." Jens Voigt.

Axams, Austria. Image - the Author

Tracciolino, the long tunnel, Italy. Image - Fritz Schwaiger

Tracciolino, Stygian adventures, Italy. Image - Fritz Schwaiger

Tracciolino, Italy. Image - Wolfgang Burghofer

Tracciolino, Italy. Image - Wolfgang Burghofer

29er – cuckoo in the nest, Novate Mezzola, Italy. Image - the Author

Spare ribbing

2013, England: As the summer closed out in Hampshire, I was pleased to note that I had more pain in my right foot than my left. I had broken it mid-way through our recent Trans-Alps. The left foot carries a thirty-year old wind-surfing injury, which is occasionally troublesome. Poor navigation, circumnavigating a coral reef in Sabah, saw me razor open the sole.

On that occasion, we were picnicking on an offshore island following a team-racing fixture at the local yacht club. I was preternaturally lucky to discover that one of our party was not only a doctor, but he was a doctor with a speedboat who worked in the casualty department of the local hospital.

Everything would have been ok if there had not been a long boozy night with dancing and high jinks to follow. Beware the prophylactic Nirvana of an opioid-based pain killer.

So, having got my most recent embarrassing injury out of the way, I guess I was as close to 100% as I ever get and ready for some other bad shit to go down. Meanwhile, I had pulled a muscle in my back, maybe chopping wood, I don't know. Anyway, that too was getting better slowly, and the stretching involved in cycling seemed to help.

However, last week I lost control on a greasy surface going moderately fast downhill on a stretch of bridleway the kids use for tobogganing in the winter. I went flying and, as luck would have it landed, not just hard, but exactly on the part of my back which had been giving me trouble. I didn't notice the broken

ribs initially. I do now. They are sore, eye-wateringly so. I got back home ok, as one usually does, but then everything seized up.

Now, what remains of my daily routine is punctuated by little squawks and squeals if I move ill-advisedly, laugh, or cough or take a deep breath. I sound like an abused puppy in a game of canine keepy-uppy, not that I have the skill for that; but I guess Samuel does.

I'm beginning to question the value of experience. When I went to take the bike out last Tuesday afternoon, I noticed the front tyre was a bit soft. So, to save a few minutes of daylight, rather than change the tube, I swapped the wheel with my old Proflex, which I had stopped using recently because the soft-compound tyres had worn slick. This is fine in dry weather, but frankly downright dangerous in winter.

Don't expect to get any smarter as you grow older. The learning curve doesn't always go up.

Cow vrs. cyclist. Image - Wolfgang Burghofer

The link from Alresford to the SDW, England. Image – the Author

One off a full house

2015, Hampshire: Now, with so many accidents resulting in broken bone accidents over the years, I sometimes suspect that I have been condemned serve out my remaining time on this planet as the village idiot. Well, it is what it is and if it's that, this salutary tale may be pointless.

It was a fine spring day out on the South Downs Way. I was just beginning to enjoy myself when I caught sight of a straggle of long-distance walkers trudging up the hill towards me. It was a fair-sized group of about 7 or 8 hikers of about my own age.

They all moved dutifully across to my left. It's gratifying that some folks still remember the advice of the Highway Code from their schooldays with the Tufty Club. This is as rare on the highways and byways of rural England as gold paving.

I slowed down and delivered a cheery greeting. But here's the thing; the group were chatting as they walked and one guy, with his head down, had merely followed the conversation and not the rationale as his companions stepped aside. However, he hadn't actually seen me. Then for reasons unknown, he moved to his left and dizzied directly into my path.

I wasn't going fast, but I was freewheeling down-hill with nowhere to go. I braked hard, my front wheel locked, and I went flying. It was a chalk trail with rocky patches. As luck would have it, I landed full-face on a flint outcrop – the same flint that attracted stone-age communities to the South Downs where they fashioned hammers and axe-heads with all the

270

material properties of tempered steel. My new friends later told me that my neck bent back at 90 degrees.

Usually, in these situations, injuries do not hurt very much initially. Immediate emotions are of befuddlement – shock and surprise. Then adrenaline kicks in. A minute or two passed before I could move. I sat up painfully, surrounded by a circle of anxious-looking ramblers, all gazing down. I felt I should at least berate the idiot J-walker, but they were all so concerned. The women, in particular, were so helpful that my anger just evaporated.

The group were well-equipped, as long-distance walkers always are. They brought out their first-aid kit, cleaned the grit from my wounds and mopped the blood from my face. They waited and stayed with me until I could get back on the bike. It was just 10kms to get home, but it was a long 10 kilometres back to Alresford that afternoon.

I dumped the bike in the garage and made a forlorn attempt to rearrange my snaggle-toothed tusks in the mirror. Then I crawled into bed, where Alison discovered me, deaf to reason, when she returned home a few hours later. Next day, she hauled me off to the local surgery, where they promptly redirected us to the district hospital.

My X-ray guy was a keen cyclist and told me that next time I should just slam right into them! The final damage racked up: right arm – broken radius; left arm – broken metacarpal, bruised ribs, loosened teeth, sliced up mouth, face flensed. Then there was something strange with the nose, and various gouges, cuts and bruises.

Alison was not happy about this, especially as we had a walking holiday in Tuscany booked to start just a week later. But as a species we have evolved to put mind over matter, so off we went off to Italy. It was not straightforward. I had grown

a week's worth of stubble to finesse my crusty facial appearance. Both arms were in slings, one was bandaged and strapped across my chest in a sling and one was in plaster. The grim-faced team at Gatwick Airport security were unsympathetic. They saw all this crepe and plaster as ruse to conceal weapons and hijack the aeroplane.

Walking was ok, but keeping my balance was not so easy. On the third day, on the strada bianca, I turned an ankle. It blew up like a melon. That now had to be strapped up too. It was getting close to a full house. And that came shortly afterwards. Capping a bittersweet holiday of soup and suppliance, our taxi to the airport was involved in a road accident. How wonderfully demonstrative are the Italians in such situations!

The South Down crash remained a mystery for months. I ignored the jinxed Pro-flex and used other bikes. The Pro-flex has a unique parallelogram fork, with a single Rise Racing shock unit in the centre. It is the stiffest fork ever made, but it is not idiot proof. When I finally had a look at it, I found that a slight loss of air-pressure over the summer meant that the fork bridge now made contact with the front tyre on full compression.

I increased the pressure, changed to a smaller tyre and got back on the bike, albeit with some misgivings. Six months later, when I replaced the headset, I found I now had masses of tyre clearance. I can only assume that back in 2009, the bike shop in Indonesia had assigned the stacks in the wrong order. I had been riding a death-trap for six years.

On the plus side, my new dentist, a charming young lady from Helensburgh, seems to have saved my front teeth.

New ways to get into trouble

2017, Hampshire: Over the years, in the course of my work, I have faced revolutions, riots, mindless sectarian bombings and civil war, with varying degrees of contrived nonchalance, growing apprehension and occasional blind panic.

Back home in England, each autumn, I brave the shooting season, as parties of braying buffoons, on the team by virtue of their net worth rather than their marksmanship, take to the South Downs with priceless Purdy shotguns. So far, I have not been shot. Yesterday, that fine record was in jeopardy.

I was riding on the South Downs Way near Winchester when, for some reason, it seemed like a good idea to include a loop along the margins of the British Army's Winchester Live Firing Range.

There is no shortage of big yellow-and-black-striped signs warning about the potential hazards of traversing the area when red flags are flying. The flagpoles extend well above the tree canopy and the flags are very large and very red. You can see them for miles. Unfortunately, when you are barrelling along a bridleway, right underneath them, they are not quite so visible.

Somewhere, in my subconscious, I could hear gunfire in the distance, but it sounded like clay-pigeon shooting, so there were no alarm bells ringing. I was riding fast on rough ground over rocks and roots and concentrating on that – all great fun. One of the downsides of having Tinnitus is that, when you exercise hard, you don't hear so well. It can be a bit of a cocoon.

This is good for focus on the task in hand, not so good for overall awareness.

Half-a-mile further on, I glanced up and saw huge red flag like the one in Tiananmen Square. Clearly, I was about to cycle into a live firing exercise; time to turn back, perhaps? But, as I retraced my route, I became aware that the gunfire was encroaching and closer than I had first thought – and it was getting louder and louder with every pedal-stroke. Worse still, this was the solid crump of bruised air. These were proper combat weapons. Shit! I pedalled for all I was worth, but the fusillade stayed right with me for an eternity.

It took a while to sink in but when, eventually, the guns faded into the distance I saw the first red flag which I had failed to notice on my way in – hanging limply. So, it seems that I had ridden right through the range and then, to compound the felony, right back through it again.

I guess that the danger is only from the odd stray bullet but, even so, the adrenaline stayed with me for the rest of the ride, and I could still see the bloody red flags flying in the far distance across two valleys.

Chasing shadows on the South Downs, England. Image - the Author

Pit-stop, Dachstein, Austria. Image - Fritz Schwaiger

275

Dachstein, Austria. Image - the Author

Dachstein Red

2017, Austria: Through the spring, we discussed another Trans-Alps bike ride. There is a superb route through the Dolomites we all want to do. Unfortunately, not everyone could make it, as alternative holidays had already been booked and families, it seems, have a vote too. An intermediate route was suggested that could be completed over a long weekend.

The Dachstein Tour circumnavigates the highest mountains in Upper Austrian. There are 'blue', 'red' and 'black' routes. The black route merely adds a couple of cul-de-sacs, where the tightly knit contours suggest pushing up hills and walking down them, so we opted for the red which retains all the good bits.

'Dachstein' is also associated with the boiled-wool, oiled-mittens of the same name. Many years ago, these excellent mitts kept my hands warm sailing from Uruguay to Australia through the icy gales and bitter snowstorms of the Southern Ocean.

For this ride, a new member was inducted into the honourable company of Fat Tired Fabulists. Fritz's younger brother Alfred would come along in place of the absent Steffen. It was a blow to discover that 'young' Alf was considerably fitter than we expected. But he made up for that by not rubbing it in our faces. And then, not only did he write up the trip, but he also built us a whole damn website! Thanks Alfred.

Fritz met me at Innsbruck Airport and, dispensing with the trolley, carried my bike bag to the car. As all my gear was in

there too it was no doubt a fair bit heavier than he expected. But, as these Austrian mountain men are (as we have already observed in these pages) legendary tough guys, I left him to it.

Fritz's partner Erika was already in Wagrain, where we would start our tour. This gave us the opportunity to have a few reunion beers on the roof-top terrace at Axams, without the distraction of dressing for dinner. Much later, we wandered off down the hill for an Italian meal. where the owner regaled us with stories of feeding his great chum, Tony Blair on his old gig at Davos. Whether we should be feeding the 'Tony Blairs' or not is another matter (apologies for the rhyming slang).

Next morning, I assembled the Merlin and we embarked on a warm-up ride from Axams to the Maria Waldrast Monastery. This is one of the highest pilgrimage routes in Austria, but God was clearly unimpressed by our devotion. He made no attempt to lift the mild hangover that left me panting in Fritz's wake. Nevertheless, it is a fine ride and varied route giving us a return trip of 56km with 1,735 metres of climbing to loosen our legs.

Next morning, marginally less hungover, we drove the 250 kilometres to Wagrain in less than the time it takes to read this paragraph. Erika has a chalet high on the hill at Weberlandl. We intended to start the tour from there. Wolfgang and Alfred arrived at the chalet the next morning in a cloud of dust, and shower of gravel; Wolfgang having overslept as usual.

The weather forecast was discouraging, but the sun was shining as we shot off along the well-graded gravel roads below the chalet. The initial route would take us down to the valley floor where we would follow bikeways for 25 kilometres to the start of the waymarked Dachstein circumnavigation at Filzmoos.

The smooth run in gave us a good look at the spectacular Dachsteingebirge. The mountain range is 50 kilometres long, but appears from nowhere, rearing up to spectacular snow-

covered peaks touching 3,000 metres. It wasn't immediately obvious how we would ride around the foothills over the next few days.

After buying some chocolate and bananas at Filzmoos the first stage to Ramsau was a mix of good 'family' bike-trails. We were impatient to engage with the mountain, but the waymarked route led us in the opposite direction, south into the Fastenberg forests. Everywhere here, there are smooth asphalted trails built at great expense as a summer training ground for cross-country skiers. The langlaufers spend their holidays rolling around recklessly on super-sized rollerblades.

In our enthusiasm, we hadn't check off the signage carefully enough as the morning progressed. So, we suddenly found ourselves competing for road space with super-fit guys exercising on their blades. Inevitably, we were distracted by these athletes and lost the marked route completely. This would be the first of many occasions when we had to retrace our steps.

A section of low-level trails followed, passing through Vordere Ramsau, Rössing, Weissenbach and Aich-Assach. A nice restaurant caught our eye in the centre of Assach. We sat down for lunch, but it seems that the cupboard was bare, so we left hungry and got back on our bikes.

We cycled on through the small village of Au to arrive in Pruggern where we found the Landgasthof Bierfriedlnice, a friendly inn on the banks of the Enns River where the waitress was prepared to feed us. Alfred then introduced us to his odd eating habits, ordering two different soups. Clearly, we'll have to wean him onto solid food some time.

Then we were off to Gröbming, along an easy trail beside the Enns River. At Moosheim, we left the riverbank and climbed slowly upwards on asphalt through Gröbming where the road turned to gravel. It was warm and sticky under a

cloudless sky, with a lush travel brochure landscape and a colourful scatter of traditional Austrian farmhouses.

The road leads directly into the sheer face of the mountain-range. There is no obvious pass. But, at the last moment, a narrow steep-sided gully comes into view. The winding ascent becomes ever-steeper, through the Öfen up to the Viehberg Alm. This is a serious hill which exposed a certain lack of condition among the older members of the party.

The Öfen translates as 'furnace' in English and does its best to honour the name. It was extremely hot and airless in the canyon. Some indeterminate, interminable time later, we breasted the Viehberg Alm watershed and the Viehbergalm Simeter Hütte came into view. Time for Cokes, radler and strudels of all kinds.

Thus fortified, we got back onto our bikes for the long downhill section to Bad Mitterndorf, where we intended to stay overnight. This descent is a gravel road, but extremely coarse with a lot of loose rocks. It really requires a downhill-bike, or at least a more robust vehicle than my 'extra-lite' Merlin. The steep head-angle on the XC bike makes it very twitchy and the impacts more-or-less wrecked the race forks.

We stopped for a drink by the Salza-Reservoir, where the landscape looks like a little bit of Scotland, before rolling into Bad Mitterndorf. As per our usual game-plan, we hadn't booked accommodation. Unfortunately, the tourist information bureau had already closed. The guys started out fussy and became progressively less so. Eventually, we settled for a surprisingly affordable suite at the Appartmenthotel Montana, with two vast double-bedrooms.

The view from the balcony was magnificent. In the last rays of the setting sun, the magnificent profile of the Dachstein ranged before us in all its grandeur. The sky was still cloudless,

but we knew things were about to change. Distance for the day was 106km with 2030 metres of ascent.

That evening on the terrace enjoying dinner, we looked back on pleasures of our day and pondered the problems of the following one. The weather models showed a deep front rolling across Europe and the system was scheduled to arrive in Upper Austria the next morning. The options were to spend a day lounging around in the hotel, go mud-wrangling with the bikes, or come up with something different entirely.

We chose the last option. Fritz called Erika and asked her to pick us up early next day and take us back to Wagrain. We would break the trip, rescheduling the 'end of tour party' mid-tour. It was the kind of idea only an Austrian could come up with.

So, we enjoyed an unstressed, and extremely generous, breakfast waiting for Erika to arrive. Alfred had picked up a slow puncture the day before, so we fixed that. Then we changed the tube as the bike belongs to Fritz and he doesn't like patches. I was happy with that as I scored a much better inner tube than the cheap-and-cheerful spare rubber that Fritz insisted on fitting.

This happy 'score' inspired me to deliver a gratuitous sermon on the riveting subject of Scottish Presbyterian ethics and gratuitous waste. I explained that in the hawthorn hedge-trimming season in Hampshire, I might have to deal with half-a-dozen punctures a week. There are enough rubber plantations in the Tropics already without us generating spurious demand. Patching tubes is our contribution to saving the planet.

Fritz wasn't convinced of the profligacy of his ways until he paid twice the price he expected for a new spare tube in the bike-shop later on that day.

Erika arrived, we locked our bikes in the ski-room, and set off for Weberlandl. I think we were all surprised how far it was

– 85km by road, and how long it took, with the rain hammering down like stair-rods. I guess we somehow imagined there would be a 'wormhole' back through space-time or, more prosaically, a serpent slide like the 'Snakes and Ladders' board game.

We apologised to Erika for her 170km round trip that morning. The poor lady then had to go back down the mountain once again to Wagrain village to collect Anita, Wolfgang's lovely wife, from the station. Meanwhile, the first keg of beer had already been breached. Then it was straight into 'job-well-done' schnapps. Premature self-gratification melted into an otherworldly haze of discombobulating flashbacks and flash-forwards.

Fritz's masterplan dictated a drinking cut-off at 3.30 p.m, so we set to work with a will as lunch was prepared, eaten and enjoyed. The second keg of beer was opened, and more rounds of schnapps followed to celebrate the anticipated happy ending of our tour in a few days' time. Fritz distributed T-shirts with his company logo and Alfred was ceremonially capped with the coveted Fat Tired Fabulists' team-bunnet.

Perhaps surprisingly, we were up bright and early for breakfast, but the weather had not cleared yet, so we didn't rush. Anita volunteered to accompany us back to Bad Mitterndorf in the Audi Supersportwagen. She blithely ignored Fritz's detailed instructions on how to drive the car and was obviously looking forward to burning some rubber once she had dropped off the pernickety owner.

It was still raining when we entered Bad Mitterndorf, so we opted for a digressionary second breakfast. A little bakery in the centre of the village that was open, the Cafe Steffl-Bäck, where we had coffee and pastries. We hung-out there until about ten when the satellite images on Alfred's phone began to look a little more encouraging.

We kitted-up for rain, but by the time we left the cafe, the sun had come out, so we soon had to stop and take it all off again. The forest was still steaming as we re-entered it to follow what turned out to be good trails and decent gravel roads, taking us up to the Ödensee above Kainitz by mid-day.

It was turning into a fresh, invigorating afternoon. The water-level in the Kainischtraun was high after the heavy rain and the air was sharp and fragrant. Bad Aussee, one of the most famous landscapes in Austria, rose resplendent in the sunshine to our right, as we trundled on to Bad Goisern.

At one stage, we found our way blocked by hay-bales, stacked high, and a bad-tempered sign arbitrarily banning cycling on the signposted bikeway. Grumpy avaricious landowners are not a species unique to England, apparently. Of course, we heaved our bikes over the barricade and carried on regardless.

From there, we climbed to the Pötschenhöhe, the pass that marks the border between the provinces of Styria and Upper Austria, with a short but welcome break riding on asphalt. We were tempted by the idea of a cappuccino at an inviting-looking inn, but headed straight back downhill to Bad Goisern, on a fine gravel track. It was now a bit late for lunch, but we were well-looked-after on the terrace of the Gasthof Zur Post.

Riding on to Gosau with full stomachs and empty brains, we followed the route markers into the forest and up the mountain. Quite how this happened remains a mystery, but the GPS trace shows us wandering like the Lost Tribe of Israel.

Our conclusion was that someone had been turning the signs round, just like boyhood hero, Wile E. Coyote in the Road Runner cartoons. We can only hope that the culprit suffered the same fate as the bold Coyote and found himself running like a food-mixer, hanging in mid-air over a canyon, with a long drop beneath.

After returning to the main road, we took no further chances and followed it up to the Pass Gschütt, between Upper Austria and Salzburg. We were sceptical when the next sign directed us into the forest again, but we successfully followed the road markers to reach Russbach at about six in the evening.

For once, we didn't add a hotel tour to the day's exertions, checking in directly at the Hotel-Restaurant Kirchenwirt, which the boys remembered from a circuit of Dachstein Blue in 2012 with Anita (anything but 'in tow'). We took two double-bedrooms and settled in. The day amounted to 70-odd kilometres in the saddle, with about 1800 metres of ascent.

Next morning it was cloudy initially; there was a prospect of some sunshine and we expected temperatures to remain fairly low. We talked to the staff at the Russbach cable car station for advice about the next section, ascending the Hornspitz. A little dogleg on asphalt, then a meadow path and finally we settled into a long grind on a gravel road.

This was the first day that we didn't meet groups of e-bikers. E-bikes might give the overweight and out-of-condition access to the mountains, but it is dispiriting in the extreme to be passed by a couple of guys, riding normal-looking bikes, chatting and laughing while you are at your limit and close to exhaustion. Only afterwards, did I realise all these athletes were on e-bikes. Such duplicitous and dispiriting devices should carry flashing blue lights.

The last part of the ascent to the Hornspitz was brutal. Wolfgang and Alfred upheld up the honour of the team with a magnificent effort, but eventually, they too had to dismount and push for the last few metres. From the ski-station we followed a long easy downhill section on gravel, all the way to Lindenthal. From there, the approach to Annaberg on asphalt was a welcome relief leading on to the Langeggsattel.

We raced a young jogger up the hill, but she was fast and, when we paused for a moment and a quick drink, she repassed us again; shamed, but quite legitimately on this occasion. The scenery around here is gorgeous – the unique alpine landscape of coffee-table books.

An Austrian biker closed up on us from behind and rode along shotgun for a while. He was on his way from Salzburg to Graz in Styria. He had match-stick legs, but boy was he fit. After a while we waved him on his way, then sat down for a rest.

With a little pushing, we finally made the Langeggsattel by lunchtime. But no lunch yet, however, as the trail led down again to Neufelden, Viertal and, on the other side of the valley, up again to the Marcheggsattel. That was the last ascent of our tour before dropping in to Filzmoose. It was short day with just 57km travelled and 1,762 metres climbed.

We elected to miss out the 25kms on bike-paths from Filzmoos back to Wagrain. Fritz called Anita and asked her to bring over the Audi so that we could return to Weberlandl for a late lunch. Anita was there to meet us at the roundabout, and presumably had been for some time, as the usual haze dust and reek of burning rubber had already cleared.

We lashed the four bikes on the back and took the fast road back to the chalet at Wagrain for a big lunch, a few beers and the inevitable schnapps. Overall, our long weekend in Austria gave us 289km and 7,325 metres and 50,000 calories to be replaced, so we set about doing that in style.

Russbach, Austria. Image - Wolfgang Burghofer

Rolling-stock-taking

We generally think that fat knobbly tyres will have more rolling resistance than narrow slicks – but it's not as simple as that and, sometimes, it's not even true. There is also the assumption that stiff sidewalls will deliver lower rolling resistance than thin, flexible sidewalls. That's definitely not true; in fact, that's one thing we can say for certain is completely wrong.

The most important design element in reducing rolling resistance is minimizing the energy lost through deformation, not minimizing how much tread is in contact with the ground. Note that a stiff tyre deforms almost exactly as much as a flexible tyre. The stiff sidewall structure might support a slightly higher percentage of the overall load via its 'mechanical spring' properties, adding to the 'air spring' provided by the inflated pressure, but on a bike tyre that's minimal overall.

In relation to deformation, there are two elements:

1. Deformation absorbs energy – so the more flexible the sidewall construction of a tyre, and thus the more easily it deforms, the less energy is expended. This applies even on the smoothest of roads as it is a constant and continuing process; and when considering rocky, bumpy roads when the tyre is working that much harder, the value of minimising energy-lost through deformation is obvious.

2. And all other factors being equal, wider tyre casings 'bulge' less as a percentage of their cross-section and also have a

shorter section of deflected sidewall; so fatter tyres, counter-intuitively, have lower rolling resistance. For example, a 25mm road-bike tyre will have 5% lower rolling resistance than the more common 23mm ones that I still use in summer as the Look won't accept anything bigger.

Super-thin tubes also help, but the effect is probably mostly psychological (an effect not to be dismissed entirely out of hand). Substituting latex for butyl will endow you with a few free watts of power and so will changing to tubeless tyres. However, my early experience with the latter, back when they were introduced, was not a happy one. Problems included initial seating issues and rolling them off the rim on downhill corners and in crashes. Then you are back with an inner tube as I have yet to see the mini-pump that will reseat a tubeless tyre on the trail-side.

As for tread patters: a well-designed knobbly with stiff treads which pass the load seamlessly across the blocks in contact with the ground is not necessarily going to be 'high rolling resistance'. However, the extent to which the individual blocks are a) compressing, and b) deforming the entire casing will have an impact – and this will be affected by the tyre pressure.

I can find no credible research on this but, if 'ease of deformation' is key in reducing rolling resistance, a softer compound on a stiff tread rather than vice versa, or an entirely stiff running surface might be better overall. However, cornering at high speed on asphalt soft knobbles 'walk' alarmingly, so I guess the handling issue prevails.

This came about because I felt that my £5,000 bike handled like a 'Halfords £99.99 Special' after fitting a new set of semi-slick tyres for a SDW trip, which seemed to have greater rolling resistance than the winter knobblies. By chance,

I had a second set of identical Maxxis tyres without 'armoured sidewalls' in the garage. The transformation was so much more than 200 grams per wheel that I checked out the research – and it pans out.

Off-road, the trail surface also makes a much bigger difference to efficient progress than you might imagine. I found some test results for measurements conducted on an uphill grade, 460m in length, with side-by-side road, gravel and meadow surfaces.

On a comparative index, it takes 20 watts to ride on asphalt, 40 watts to ride on grass but, unbelievably, 120 watts to cover the same ground on meadow. The fact that I often chose to ride on the grass alongside the narrow ribbon of flinty trail to look after my tyres, suggests a level of intelligence little better than the sheep who often accompany me.

Alison climbs a hill above Loch Long. Image – the Author

Tracciolino Tour, Austria. Image - Wolfgang Burghofer

Trans-Alps bikes

When you get back on a road-bike after an Alpine trip you feel like Superman. Released from the super-gravity of the Trans-Alps gear, it hardly seems necessary to pedal; you fly along on a magic-carpet of relativity, warped by your historical frame of reference.

But is it really necessary to carry all the additional weight of dual-suspension and American junk-yard engineering to Alpine cols, just to cruise down them in relative safety; then, find you can't climb and have to walk the bike back up again?

Even now, I am still unsure about the right bike for such a trip. Initially, thought it might be worth trading my mechanically endowed downhill 'skills' for the enhanced climbing ability of a light-weight hard-tail. My titanium Merlin XLM, for example, is unusually light at 9kg and comes in at 5 or 6 kg less than the dual-suspension Scott genius I used on our first Trans-Alps.

The 29ers arrived with much fanfare. These are big bikes and obviously heavier per se. Nevertheless, on my second trip, I fell for the hype and rented a Specialized FSR 29er. To be fair, the FSR was actually no heavier than the 26" Scott (14.5kg). No matter, it was still disappointing. While the FSR 29er was great downhill or on forest roads, it was hopeless for tight single-track; I hated it.

In some recent testing, there was no discernible difference between the 29" wheels currently favoured for XC racing and

the 26" wheels, now only recommended for bomb-proof long-travel suspension DH bikes. And the current all-purpose 27.5" wheel size appeared to be measurably slower than either. This makes no sense whatsoever and only shows how difficult it is to rate theoretical advantages in 'real-use' conditions.

So, whatever you read about wheel size, take it with a pinch of marketing salt. The industry only introduced 29ers to sell more bikes. Cyclists are a relentlessly targeted demographic. They may be either careful shoppers or cheapskates in the real world, but they all buy bikes like Imelda Marcos used to buy shoes.

It didn't take long before the downsides of the 29er to become apparent. Not everyone is convinced by the theoretical merits of these clumsy big bikes. The larger wheel engages rough ground with a marginally more favourable angle of attack, but you are more likely to avoid the bump altogether with the nimbler 26" wheel bike. And it's particularly irritating that the extra 9" of overall length means that your pride and joy sticks out by around 9" when carried across the back of the car on a towbar-mounted bike-rack.

But rather than admit the mistake, the industry introduced a third, intermediate, size. The 27.5" wheel is almost identical to that used on 700C road-bikes and is supposed to combine the best of both worlds. This is just complete nonsense.

While the new size is certainly more nimble than a 29er, there is almost no difference between the 27.5" and 26" wheel, even when you hit a rock. And whatever distinguishes the two, tyre choice and suspension set-up make much more impact on the handling package than wheel rim diameter.

In the days before GPS odometers, we had to roll the wheel out to calibrate distance from rotations. I was surprised to find my big wheel/small tyre road-bike and small wheel/fat

tyre mountain-bikes identical. There is clearly a sweet spot here. The 29er with fat tyres misses the sweet spot completely.

Yet another new trend homes in on this sweet spot. Gravel bikes are the next big thing. Now we have disc brakes on road-bikes, it's possible to change wheel size if you have time for all this nonsense. So, 650c rims are now mated with fat tyres to maintain the rolling diameter of the 700c with regular road tyres.

As a result of all these transparent marketing shenanigans, I thought that my Merlin XLM would be fine in the Alps. However, when I finally took it to Austria in 2017, it was absolutely hopeless. The head angle is just too steep for carefree-wheeling downhill and I was always nervous with it. Moreover, the experiment cost me a new set of forks. I comprehensively wrecked the coveted lightweight XC Rockshox that suited the South Downs perfectly.

My Austrian friends use locally-made hard-tails with a slack head angle and 2.25" tyres. They are built like the proverbial brick shithouse. However, on one occasion, when I took one of Fritz's bikes down the hill from the Adolf Pishler Hütte, I discovered that I had no steering and no brakes at the first fast bend. Robust construction in itself is clearly not enough although, in this case, the hairy handling was down to the tyres.

I guess we end up recommending a hardtail 29er for the Alps, as that is pretty much the only thing you can buy. The dual suspension frame at this size is just too damn heavy to carry. If you are small in stature, you can get the same bike with 27.5" wheels. That is better, but an old-style lightweight, dual-suspension 26" wheel bike is still better.

On the subject of gears, after my experience 'running out' of gears (at both the top and the bottom of the range) on a 2x bike with just two chain-rings, I can't believe that 1x (single front chain-ring) gear system, is really the way forward. The

front derailleur is one of the best bike inventions of all time. It ensures good chain-lines, it is easy to operate, exceptionally reliable and cheap to replace. It is simply perverse to abandon such a brilliant device.

The 1x uses a great heavy rear cluster the size of a dinner plate. The objections here are obvious. First up, the set-up looks terrible. Then the massive cluster weighs a ton, and the weight is in the wrong place on the bike. The little cogs are smaller than you would like for descending and this impacts on the life cycle of the chain and the cog itself.

The quest to achieve the same range of gearing on a 1x as a 3x is basically pushing shit uphill. For the up/down, up/down, up/down, up/down riding of the Alps, I remain less than convinced. And when you do have to replace chains (more frequent due to the bad chain lines) and rear clusters (issues concern the sheer size, complex engineering and short life) well, you might not think a 1x system is so wonderful long-term.

26″ and 29″ wheels. Image - Wolfgang Burghofer

Unsupported assertions

In the 1970s and 1980, my brother and his wife Helen used to tour Scotland on their classic, hand-made Dawes touring bikes. Reynolds 531 steel tubing, Brookes saddles and panniers – the whole 'Cyclists Touring Club' thing. They criss-crossed the backroads of Scotland and Ireland and regularly took this heavy kit with 38mm road tyres across the Cairngorms on trails that are now ridden only by mountain-bikes.

They were genuinely unsupported; they slept in tents and carried sleeping bags, cooking gear and, of course, food. This old-style riding is still popular, but it's not my thing. I ride because I love the feel of a really good bike under me. If I am more interested in the landscape than the riding experience, I hike. So, I have no interest in riding unresponsive bikes, heavy bikes or even good bikes laden down with survival gear.

My preferred style of 'unsupported riding' is sometimes characterised as 'credit card touring'. Credit cards are durable, waterproof and seal the deal by weighing nothing. Of course, you still have to carry stuff. What we discovered is that you don't need to carry much, even if you are on the road for a week. My first pack weighed 6.5kg all-up and I have got that down to less than 4kg. This lightest backpack weighs half a kilogram or so; so all this obviously requires a bit of careful planning.

Modern fabrics are light and dry quickly after rain or after washing. Mobile phones are good enough today not to require

a camera – although sometimes you do long for a decent lens. One charger will do everything if you splice up some short cables.

	Trans-Alps - rucksack items	grams
1.	Rucksack	580
2.	Spare inner tube	200
3.	Tracksuit trousers	270
4.	Tracksuit top	270
5.	Fleece pullover	300
6.	Rain jacket	150
7.	Windproof gilet	50
8.	Rain shorts (MTB baggies)	180
9.	Spare cycling jersey	180
10.	Spare cycling shorts	200
11.	Spare cycling socks	10
12.	Waterproof socks	80
13.	Neoprene gloves	60
14.	Fleece gilet	120
15.	Arm-warmers	70
16.	First aid kit	80
17.	Shampoo	40
18.	Travel toothbrush and toothpaste	30
19.	Wallet, etc	10
20.	GPS charger	100
21.	Phone and charger cable	200
22.	Spare inner tube	150
23.	Tyre boot (for cuts)	50
24.	Puncture repair kit	20
25.	Chain-break tool, Allen-keys, tyre levers, etc	60
26.	Pump	75
	Total = about 3.5kg	3,535

If you are riding in a group, not everyone needs to carry a first aid kit, pump and chain-break tool. But everyone needs to make sure they have the correct Allen-keys for their bike and at least one tube. Riding alone, you will obviously need to be entirely self-sufficient.

Most people today use tubeless tyres with sealant. I was an early adopter of tubeless and had all sorts of problems with the bead 'unseating' and sudden deflation. I am told they are better now; but, if you get a flat, or a cut in the tyre that requires a 'boot' repair, you will still need spare tubes. I have yet to meet the man who can reseat a tubeless tyre with a mini pump.

Trans-Alps items - worn

1.	Cycling jersey	180
2.	Windproof outer jersey	410
3.	Cycling shorts (¾ length)	220
4.	Socks	10
5.	Shoes	80
6.	Gloves	40
7.	Head rag	40
8.	Watch	50
9.	Helmet	260
10.	Water bottle (full)	800
11.	Energy snacks	20
12.	**Total = about 2kg**	2,110

The big-ticket item here is the water bottle. In the tropics, I used to use a Camelbak *and* carry two bottles. If you want to reduce bike weight by 2.5kg you would need to start with a pretty heavy bike and then spend about $5,000. That maybe the case, but don't believe the cynics who equate a better bike with half a litre of water. On the trail, they are not the same at all.

In the Alps you are unlucky if you find water-stops more than 'one bottle' apart. These were originally set up for hikers

in the dim and distant past who are slower and need more frequent pit stops. And we do find ourselves hiking occasionally. I initially used 'hike and bike' shoes. After I weighed them, I threw them away. You will do more biking and less hiking with MTB shoes.

Cappuccino, Tuscany, Italy. Image - Alison Spice

Tam o' Shanter

We think na on the lang Scots miles,
The mosses, waters, slaps, and styles,
That lie between us and our hame,
Tam skelpit on thro' dub and mire;
Despisin' wind and rain and fire.

Where sits our sulky sullen dame.
Gathering her brows like gathering storm,
Nursing her wrath to keep it warm.
She tauld thee weel thou was a skellum,
A blethering, blustering, drunken blellum

Whiles holding fast his gude blue bonnet;
Whiles crooning o'er some auld Scots sonnet.[2]

---

[2] Lines extracted from the narrative poem 'Tam o' Shanter' by Robert Burns; re-purposed as an ode to the late-returning cyclist.

* fat-tired fabulists *

.....in search of Hannibal.....

http://www.fat-tired-fabulists.com/en/startseite/

The Piper Calls the Tune is an account of the life and works of David Boyd (1902-1989), a significant and highly regarded yacht designer, who experienced both great success and great frustration through his 60-year career. The book reviews Boyd's contribution to the maritime heritage of the Clyde Estuary and celebrates his enduring legacy.

The Piper Calls the Tune is a nostalgic insight into a wonderful world of inspired designers, beautiful yachts, eccentric owners and skilled craftsmen. It records the memories of a generation of proud old men who have been pleased to revisit the golden age they experienced, before it is swept away in the revisionist accounts of today that sometimes seem to focus only on Fife, Watson and Charles E. Nicholson.

Available post-free from Amazon USA, Europe and UK.

Sailing is arguably the most diverse and multifaceted of all leisure pursuits, thus it is also perhaps the sport most richly endowed with specialist literature. Consequently, countless well-researched histories of yachting have been published since Victorian times. However, unaccountably, not one has focussed on Scotland. While individual Scottish designers have been lauded, even lionised, in lush biographies, the wider story of sailing in Scotland has been marginalised.

Highland Cowes views yachting history 'through the lens' of Hunter's Quay – the heart of sailing in Scotland during the 'golden age of yachting'. The narrative seeks to identify gaps in the pantheon and to slot in lesser known, but no less worthy, figures who are now brought stage centre.

Available post-free from Amazon USA, Europe and UK.

Austrian Barman. Image – the Author

303

Printed in Great Britain
by Amazon